Best Easy Day Hikes Series

Best Easy Day Hikes
Washington, D.C.

Louise S. Baxter

FALCONGUIDES

GUILFORD, CONNECTICUT
HELENA, MONTANA

FALCONGUIDES®

Copyright © 2011 by Rowman & Littlefield

FalconGuides is an imprint of Globe Pequot Press.
Falcon, FalconGuides, and Outfit Your Mind are registered trademarks of Rowman & Littlefield.

TOPO! Explorer software and SuperQuad source maps courtesy of National Geographic Maps. For information about TOPO! Explorer, TOPO!, and Nat Geo Maps products, go to www .topo .com or www .natgeomaps.com.

Maps by Design Maps Inc. © Rowman & Littlefield
Layout: Kevin Mak
Project editor: Gregory Hyman

Library of Congress Cataloging-in-Publication Data is available on file.

ISBN 978-0-7627-6059-6

Printed in the United States of America

Distributed by NATIONAL BOOK NETWORK

Contents

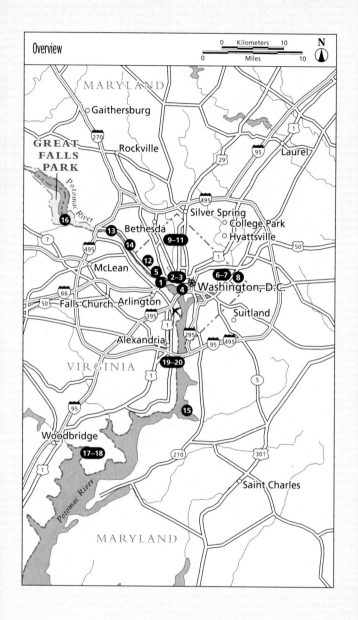

Acknowledgments

Many thanks to my friends, who gave me great ideas for hikes and supported me throughout this process. A special thanks to my brother, Craig, who has always believed in me. I want to express my great appreciation for the National Park Service, Virginia State Parks, and private preservation organizations that do a wonderful job of making sure that we understand the importance, historically and environmentally, of the parklands they protect. It is because of them that we will enjoy these areas for years to come.

Introduction

Washington, D.C., is a designed city, mostly urban and residential, without a lot of wild areas. That said, however, there are many opportunities for hiking and getting back to nature. The city's biggest park, Rock Creek Park, has many trails and outdoor activities. The C&O Canal begins its 185-mile run in Georgetown and a towpath follows the entire route; and the Potomac River is flanked with walking trails on the Washington, D.C.; Maryland; and Virginia sides. Being the nation's capital means that much of the land here is federally owned and protected for monuments and memorials, and for environmental preserves. Part of the city is built on what was once swampland, so water plays a big part in the natural ecosystem of the area. Marshes and wetlands abound along the river.

Washington, D.C., was designed on a grid system, with lettered streets running east–west and numbered streets running north–south. The US Capitol is the center of the city and from it four sections are created: Northwest (NW), Southwest (SW), Northeast (NE), and Southeast (SE). That's why every address in Washington has one of these suffixes on it. To make things more interesting, however, diagonal avenues named for states pierce through the grid, creating squares and circles. But what the city loses in easy navigation it gains in beauty, as many of these squares and circles provide opportunities to honor history and make some green space. Ironically, the city was designed this way to prevent enemy armies from finding easy access to important buildings. The British, however, in 1814, had no trouble getting in and burning both the White House and the US Capitol. So the plan really only serves to confuse those trying to get around today. Best advice: Carry a good map and be patient.

Weather

Washington, D.C., is in the mid-Atlantic region, which has a humid climate. The area is known for its hot and sticky summers and, generally, mild winters, with roughly a foot of snow accumulated through the season. While every hike in this book can be done throughout the year, spring and fall usually offer comfortable temperatures and are the ideal times for hiking. In summer try to walk in the morning or evening. Trails, especially those that follow the river or the canal, can get buggy, so bring insect repellent. The sun can be strong too, even in winter, so wear sunscreen on trails that are out in the open. These hikes are designed for all levels of ability; generally a good pair of sneakers is enough to navigate the trails.

Traffic

The Washington, D.C. metro area boasts some of the worst traffic in the country! That said, it's still a great place to live and visit. Just be aware and plan a little extra time to get around. Also, many roads have strict rush-hour restrictions on weekdays, except major holidays—in particular I-66, Canal Road, and Rock Creek Parkway.

- I-66 inside the Beltway (I-495) is HOV-2 (a high-occupancy vehicle lane; at least two persons in car) inbound (east toward Washington) from 6:30 a.m. to 9 a.m. and outbound (west from Washington, D.C.) from 4 p.m. to 6 p.m.

- Canal Road is one way going south from 6:15 a.m. to 10 a.m. and one way going north from 2:45 p.m. to 7:15 p.m.
- Rock Creek Parkway is one way going south from 6:45 a.m. to 9:30 a.m. and one way going north from 3:45 p.m. to 6:30 p.m.

It's best to avoid those streets on weekdays before 10 a.m. and after 4 p.m. If you find yourself in these areas during rush-hour times, be sure to have a map handy for detour routes. Washington, D.C.–area public transportation information for Metrorail and Metrobus can be found at www.wmata.com. Some of the trailheads in this guide are accessible via public transportation; when they are, the corresponding route is included with the hike description.

Leave No Trace

Most of the trails in this book are maintained by governmental or private organizations and are well taken care of. Please take care when you visit to preserve the areas for others.

- Stay on the designated trails. Many off-trail areas are not safe or they may be in the process of revegetation projects.
- Don't leave anything behind; pack your trash and discard it in a trash receptacle, if available, or take it with you when you leave the park.
- Be careful of wild animals and don't feed them.
- Leave flowers, rocks, and other "souvenirs" behind. Take only pictures and memories.

- Be mindful of other users on the trails. Many trails are used by cyclists; listen for the familiar "On your left" warning and move to the right to let them pass.

- Keep your noise level at a minimum. Shouting can be startling to wildlife and other humans.

- Dogs are permitted on most of the trails. They must be on leashes no longer than 6 feet. Please pick up after them.

- Please do not smoke on the trails. It's not expressly prohibited, but can mar the enjoyment of other trail users.

Safety

The trails featured here are short and, often, near populated areas where help is readily available. However, it's best to be prepared.

- Always carry water. Especially in the summer, humidity can take its toll on the body and dehydration is a danger.

- There is cell service available from most of the trails. Carry a phone with you in case of emergency. But keep it on vibrate or a low ring so others aren't disturbed.

- Carry a basic first-aid kit including antiseptic and bandages for scrapes.

- Watch out for poison ivy. It grows well in this area and is often seen along the trails. If you stay on the trails, you should be able to avoid it.

How to Use This Guide

This guide is designed to give concise information about the area of each hike and answer common questions about each trail. Each hike description provides the total distance of the route, along with a detailed breakdown of distances between landmarks and directions to reach them. Admission fees and times, type of trail surface, other trail users, and additional helpful information is listed with each hike. Park websites are also given; it's a good idea to check these ahead of time in case there are any special events or closures when you are planning to visit.

The hikes in this guide were chosen for their accessibility, easy ability levels, and scenic and historical values. Some are in very wooded, natural areas, while others are along paved paths following the water or historic sites.

Parking in Washington, D.C., is not always easy. Most of the trailheads purposely are located at places with ample parking. As anywhere, weekends tend to be busier than weekdays. Two hikes start at the Smithsonian Metro stop. Parking along the National Mall is available, but can be difficult to find. Some hike descriptions include information on public transportation, which usually involves a combination of Metrorail and Metrobus routes, or Metrorail and additional walking time.

Please be aware of any special events that might be going on when you want to go for a hike. You can find out about what's going on by visiting the Washington, D.C. visitor center at www.washington.org.

Selecting a Hike

These are all easy hikes, but easy is a relative term. The ratings provided with each hike description should help you decide which trail best suits your needs and abilities.

- **Easy** hikes are generally short and flat, taking no longer than an hour or two to complete.
- **Moderate** hikes involve increased distance and relatively mild changes in elevation, and will take two hours or more to complete.

Keep in mind that what you think is easy is entirely dependent on your level of fitness and the adequacy of your gear (primarily shoes). Use the trail's length as a gauge of its relative difficulty—even if climbing is involved, it won't be bad if the hike is less than 1 mile long. If you are hiking with a group, select a hike that is appropriate for the least fit and prepared person in your party.

Approximate hiking times are based on the assumption that on flat ground, most walkers average 2 miles per hour. For a ballpark hiking duration, adjust that rate by the steepness of the terrain, your level of fitness (subtract time if you're used to exercise and add time if you're hiking with kids), and any time you'll spend taking photographs or strolling through museums or gardens.

Trail Finder

Best Hikes for History Buffs

Best Hikes for Nature Lovers

Best Hikes for Water Views

Best Hikes for Environmentalists

Best Hikes for Gardeners

Map Legend

	Interstate Highway
	U.S. Highway
	State Highway
	Local Road
	Unpaved Road
	Featured Trail
	Trail
	Paved Trail
	River/Creek
	Local/State Park
	National Forest
	Marsh/Swamp
	Body of Water
✈	Airport
‖‖‖‖‖	Boardwalk
⌣	Bridge
●—●	Gate
⌖	Lighthouse
M	Metro Station
▲	Mountain/Peak
P	Parking
⊞	Picnic Area
■	Point of Interest/Structure
⊞	Restroom
○	Town
⑪	Trailhead
⬕	Viewpoint/Overlook
❓	Visitor/Information Center
⬚	Water

Historical Washington

1 Theodore Roosevelt Island

Any talk about hiking around the Washington, D.C. area has to start at Theodore Roosevelt Island. The entire island is a memorial to the twenty-sixth president, an avid conservationist and the founder of the national park system.

Distance: 2.4-mile lollipop
Approximate hiking time: 1.5 hours
Difficulty: Easy
Trail surface: Smooth dirt path and boardwalks
Best seasons: Year-round
Other trail users: Hikers only
Canine compatibility: Leashed dogs permitted
Fees and permits: None

Schedule: Daily from 6 a.m. to 10 p.m.
Maps: National Park Service maps are at www.nps.gov/this
Trail contact: Theodore Roosevelt Island, c/o Turkey Run Park, George Washington Memorial Parkway, McLean, VA 22101; (703) 289-2500; www.nps.gov/this

Finding the trailhead: By car: The parking lot is only accessible from the George Washington Parkway heading north. Just after the Roosevelt Bridge, look for the parking area on the right. **Via Metro:** Take the Blue or the Orange line to Rosslyn. From the station, walk along Moore Street to 19th Street. Turn right and then left on Lynn Street and follow the path to the right, which leads to a bridge crossing the George Washington Parkway. This will bring you to the parking lot for Roosevelt Island. The trailhead is at the south end of the parking lot by the pedestrian bridge. GPS: N38 53.860' / W77 04.058'

The Hike

This natural island in the Potomac is directly across from Georgetown and the Washington Harbour and, although it can only be accessed from Virginia, it is part of the District of Columbia. A footbridge connects the parking lot to the island, affording nice views of the spires of Georgetown University and the towers of the National Cathedral off to the left.

The island was purchased by the Theodore Roosevelt Memorial Association in 1931 and was dedicated as the official memorial in 1967. The island is predominantly maintained as a natural area as a tribute to Roosevelt, who was an avid outdoorsman and naturalist.

The hike winds around the island, beginning on the Swamp Trail, which leads to the south end of the island near the Roosevelt Bridge. At this point, the trail becomes a boardwalk through the swamp area, a tidal marsh where the water levels rise and fall with the tides. Crayfish can be found in the swamp and are a favorite of the raccoons. Keep an eye out for deer; quite a few have come to live on the island in recent years.

After the boardwalk ends, be sure to take a short detour down to the river's edge. To the left you can see Key Bridge. Directly across the river is the Washington Harbour area, and to the right the Watergate Complex and the Kennedy Center for the Performing Arts. On a nice day, expect to see kayaks, canoes, and rowboats on the water.

In the center of the island is a large open plaza with a 17-foot statue of Roosevelt surrounded by stone slabs with some of his quotations about manhood, youth, nature, and the nation. The plaza is surrounded by benches and a moat with fountains, providing a cool spot to relax before continuing on the hike.

The island is a convenient getaway for urbanites who want to experience some unspoiled nature. But you will

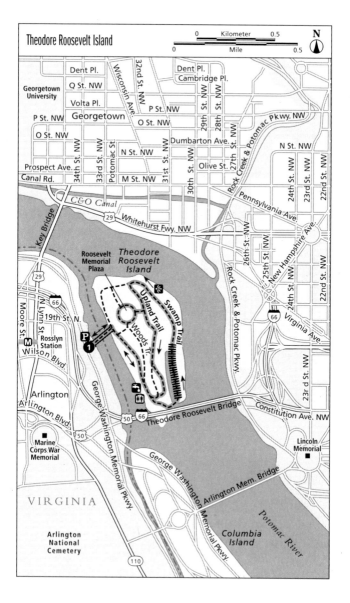

know you're not far from the city as the planes coming in to land at nearby Ronald Reagan Washington National Airport fly right above.

Miles and Directions

0.0 Begin by crossing the pedestrian bridge from the parking lot.

0.1 At the entrance to the island, turn right and follow the far right trail, the Swamp Trail.

0.3 Continue straight; the Woods Trail ends here. Just ahead are restrooms and a drinking fountain.

0.5 The trail bears left at the south end of the island just under the Roosevelt Bridge. The path becomes a boardwalk.

0.7 Turn left to walk the short boardwalk to the middle of the swamp. Return to the main path.

1.0 Just after the boardwalk ends, there is a narrow unmarked trail that goes right. Follow this for views of the water and the Washington Harbour across the river. The trail will loop around and rejoin the Swamp Trail.

1.1 Bear right to stay on the trail. When it divides, turn left to join the Upland Trail.

1.2 Turn right to go into memorial plaza.

1.3 Arrive at memorial plaza. After visiting, return to the Upland Trail and turn right.

1.7 At the fork, bear left and continue on the Upland Trail.

2.0 The Upland Trail ends at the Swamp Trail where the restrooms and drinking fountain are. Turn right and retrace your steps to the island entrance.

2.3 Turn left to cross the bridge back to the parking lot.

2.4 Arrive back at the trailhead and the parking lot.

2 Monuments and Memorials

From the Washington Monument to the Lincoln Memorial, the west side of the National Mall is a walk through history. Visit these honored sites and discover a few surprises along the way.

Distance: 2.6-mile loop
Approximate hiking time: 3 hours, including time viewing the memorials
Difficulty: Easy
Trail surface: Smooth clay path
Best seasons: Year-round
Other trail users: Runners, sightseers
Canine compatibility: Leashed dogs permitted
Fees and permits: None
Schedule: The National Mall is always open. Monuments and memorials are lit up at night until midnight; visitor centers are open during business hours.
Maps: National Park Service mall map at www.nps.gov/nama. Maps can also be picked up at kiosks by the Washington Monument and the Lincoln Memorial.
Trail contact: National Mall and Memorial Parks, 900 Ohio Dr. SW, Washington, D.C. 20024; (202) 426-6841; www.nps.gov/nama

Finding the trailhead: By car: Take I-66 east or US 50 east and cross the Roosevelt Bridge. Stay straight and continue on Constitution Avenue. Follow this to 15th Street and turn right. Get in the left lane and turn left at Jefferson Drive SW. Park anywhere along the street. (**Note:** There are meters and a time limit is enforced. Parking is not allowed during rush hours—between 6:30 a.m. and 9:30 a.m. and between 4 p.m. and 6:30 p.m.) Start the hike near the Metro stop indicated by a brown pole. **Via Metro:** Take the Blue or Orange line to the Smithsonian stop. Exit toward the National Mall and start the hike at the top of the escalator by the brown Metro pole. GPS: N38 53.318' / W77 01.701'

The Hike

Certainly the most-recognized structure in the capital city is the 555-foot-high Washington Monument, built to honor the nation's first president. You will notice that about one-third of the way up the monument, the color of the marble changes slightly. The construction began in 1848, but was halted during the Civil War. When the builders returned in the 1870s to the same quarry for more marble, enough time had passed to change the color slightly, creating this unusual mark on the obelisk. To ride to the top of the monument, free tickets can be acquired through the National Park Service.

As you continue past the monument, walk down a hill to the World War II Memorial. Dedicated in 2004, this expansive site pays tribute to those who fought and died in that war. The memorial is surrounded by fifty-six pillars, which represent the District of Columbia and the US states and US territories existing at the time of the war. In the center is a large fountain, a perfect place to sit, especially on a hot day.

From the World War II Memorial, walk along the far right side of the mall (not along the reflecting pool) toward the Lincoln Memorial. On your left will be a small lake. Turn left at the marked entrance to Constitution Gardens, taking the path that leads to a small island in the lake. Dedicated during the bicentennial, the island displays fifty-six stones, each with an etched replica of a signature on the Declaration of Independence. Constitution Gardens provides a quiet respite from the busy mall and is a cool spot in the hot summer.

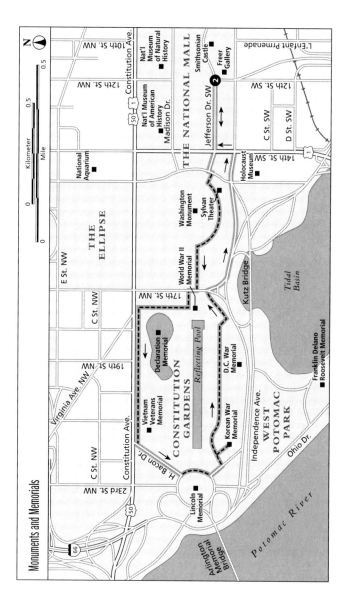

Monuments and Memorials

Return to the path and turn left toward the Vietnam Veterans Memorial on your left. Walk past this somber wall that lists the name of each person killed in the conflict. At the end is a statue of three servicemen.

From the Vietnam memorial you can walk straight to the Lincoln Memorial. The structure is surrounded by thirty-six columns, representing the thirty-six states in the Union at the time of Lincoln's death, and inscribed on the interior walls are some of his speeches, including the most famous Gettysburg Address. Spend some time here with the large seated statue of the sixteenth president. Lincoln was a great advocate for the deaf, and, if you look closely, you can see that his hands are displaying the sign language letters "A" and "L." From the Lincoln Memorial steps, many notable speeches and rallies have taken place; perhaps most famous is Martin Luther King's "I Have a Dream" speech.

Head to the right of the steps toward the Korean War Memorial. Nineteen statues of soldiers of many races stand as if they are marching up a hill and these statues are reflected on a granite wall, creating thirty-eight soldiers representing the Thirty-Eighth Parallel. The wall is etched with the faces of many who contributed to the war effort, including nurses, doctors, and clerks.

Continue on the path back toward the Washington Monument. Pass by the Sylvan Theater, where free concerts and plays are offered throughout the summer. Cross the monument grounds and 15th and 14th Streets and return to the Metro stop and trailhead.

Miles and Directions

0.0 Start at the Smithsonian Metro stop on the National Mall. Walk toward the Washington Monument.

0.3 From the Washington Monument, walk west toward the World War II Memorial.

0.7 Turn left into Constitution Gardens and return to the path. Turn left.

1.1 Bear slightly left to visit the Vietnam Veterans Memorial.

1.3 Arrive at the Lincoln Memorial.

2.6 Arrive back at the Smithsonian Metro stop and the trailhead.

3 Museums and Gardens

Walking around the east side of the mall, pass by several Smithsonian museums and through sculpture and botanic gardens on this short, easy tour.

Distance: 2.4-mile loop
Approximate hiking time: 3 hours, including stops at the sculpture gardens and the US Botanic Garden; more if you spend time in any of the museums
Difficulty: Easy
Trail surface: Smooth clay path; some sidewalks
Best seasons: Year-round
Other trail users: Runners, sightseers
Canine compatibility: Leashed dogs permitted. Dogs not allowed inside museums or gardens.
Fees and permits: None
Schedule: The National Mall is always open. Museums and gardens are open at varying times; check specific websites for hours.
Maps: National Park Service maps at www.nps.gov/nama
Trail contact: National Mall and Memorial Parks, 900 Ohio Dr. SW, Washington, D.C. 20024; (202) 426-6841; www.nps.gov/nama

Finding the trailhead: By car: Take I-66 east or US 50 east and cross the Roosevelt Bridge. Stay straight and continue on Constitution Avenue. Follow this to 15th Street and turn right. Get in the left lane and turn left at Jefferson Drive SW. Park anywhere along the street. (**Note:** There are parking meters and a time limit is enforced. Parking is not allowed during rush hours—between 6:30 a.m. and 9:30 a.m. and between 4 p.m. and 6:30 p.m.) Start the hike near the Metro stop indicated by a brown pole. **Via Metro:** Take the Blue or the Orange line to the Smithsonian stop. Exit toward the National Mall and start the hike at the top of the escalator by the brown Metro pole. GPS: N38 53.318' / W77 01.701'

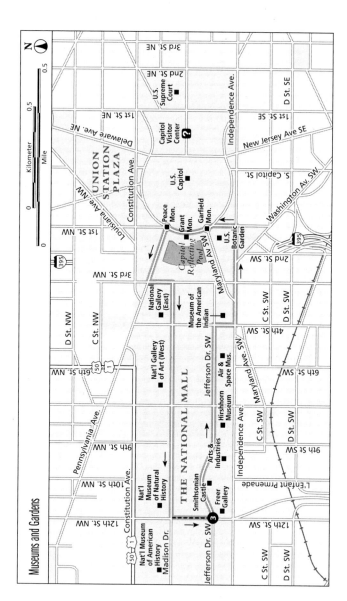

Museums and Gardens

N

0   Kilometer   0.5
0   Mile   0.5

3rd St. NE
2nd St. NE
U.S. Supreme Court
1st St. NE
Delaware Ave. NE
Capitol Visitor Center ?
D St. SE
1st St. SE
Independence Ave.
New Jersey Ave SE
U.S. Capitol
S. Capitol St.
Washington Ave. SW
UNION STATION PLAZA
Constitution Ave.
Louisiana Ave. NW
Peace Mon. Grant Mon. Garfield Mon.
1st St. NW
Capitol Reflecting Pool
U.S. Botanic Garden
Maryland AV SW
2nd St. SW
395
3rd St. NW
National Gallery (East)
Museum of the American Indian
C St. SW
D St. SW
D St. NW
C St. NW
Nat'l Gallery of Art (West)
Jefferson Dr. SW
Air & Space Mus.
4th St. SW
Maryland Ave. SW
6th St. NW
50 1
THE NATIONAL MALL
Hirshhorn Museum
Independence Ave.
6th St SW
C St. SW
D St. SW
Pennsylvania Ave.
9th St. NW
Arts & Industries
L'Enfant Promenade
9th St SW
10th St. NW
Nat'l Museum of Natural History
Smithsonian Castle
Freer Gallery
Jefferson Dr. SW
12th St. NW
Constitution Ave.
Nat'l Museum of American History
Madison Dr.
50 1
C St. SW
D St. SW
12th St. SW

The Hike

Begin at the Smithsonian Metro stop and turn right toward the Freer and Sackler Galleries. These house Asian art and some American collections. Walk along the mall on the clay path. This portion of the National Mall is home to the Smithsonian Folklife Festival, held at the end of June. The festival focuses on three different cultures every year and highlights the various art forms of each one, including dance, music, and cuisine. The red building on your right is the Smithsonian Castle, which houses the offices of the institute. Farther along, in front of the original Smithsonian Museum, the Arts and Industries Building, is an old-fashioned carousel.

Continue on, then leave the path at the entrance to the Hirshhorn Museum and Sculpture Garden. The garden is below street level and features works of contemporary art situated around a small reflecting pool. Exit the garden at the far end and rejoin the clay path. Walk past the National Air and Space Museum and, at 4th Street, turn right at the National Museum of the American Indian. This museum is the newest on the mall and has one of the best museum cafeterias. Foods from the many native regions, in both North and South America, are available.

From the Museum of the American Indian, walk up to Independence Avenue. Turn left and walk to 1st Street and turn left. One of the oldest in the nation, the US Botanic Garden displays plants of historical and environmental significance. Take a stroll through desert, rain forest, and lush foliage in the different rooms. The gardens offer special programs including yoga, cooking classes, and plant education classes.

Walk along 1st Street, right in front of the US Capitol. This is the west side of the building; as you face it the House of Representatives is on the right and the Senate is on the left. The statue of Freedom stands atop the dome. Walk along the Reflecting Pool, then turn left on Pennsylvania Avenue, left on 3rd Street, and right at Madison Drive, heading back down the mall.

Walk through the National Gallery of Art's sculpture garden. This garden also features modern art, including a giant typewriter eraser and a leaning stack of chairs. There is a pond in the middle of the garden that, in winter, is used as a skating rink; the rest of the year, it has a fountain.

Follow the path past the National Museum of Natural History, where you can see the Hope Diamond or catch a movie at the IMAX Theater. Just beyond is the National Museum of American History. This was once called "The Nation's Attic," as it is where you can find objects of American cultural history such as Julia Child's kitchen and Hank Aaron's baseball glove. The recently restored American flag that flew over Fort McHenry and inspired the "Star-Spangled Banner" is in the main hall. From here, return to the trailhead and Metro stop.

Miles and Directions

0.0   Start at the Smithsonian Metro stop. Walk east, toward the US Capitol, along the right side of the mall area.

0.6   Turn right onto 4th Street right by the Museum of the American Indian. Then turn left onto Independence Avenue.

0.9   At the corner of 1st Street and Independence Avenue, turn left and, if you wish to, visit the US Botanic Garden. Continue on 1st Street, crossing in front of the US Capitol. Turn left on Pennsylvania Avenue, then left on 3rd Street.

1.2   At Madison Drive, turn right and follow the path on the mall.

2.4   Return to the trailhead and the Smithsonian Metro stop.

4 Tidal Basin and Hains Point

This pristine walk starts and ends along the Tidal Basin, with visits to the FDR and Jefferson Memorials. It follows the Potomac River out to the Hains Point peninsula, with views of the Potomac River on one side and the Washington Channel on the other.

Distance: 5.4-mile lollipop
Approximate hiking time: 4 hours, including stops at the memorials
Difficulty: Moderate
Trail surface: Paved walkways
Best seasons: Year-round
Other trail users: Runners, cyclists
Canine compatibility: Leashed dogs permitted

Fees and permits: None
Schedule: Open all day, every day
Maps: National Park Service maps at www.nps.gov/nama. Maps can also be picked up at kiosks by the FDR Memorial and the Jefferson Memorial. Also see Rand McNally Washington DC Metro Street Guide: page 103; B7, C7, D8, E8.

Finding the trailhead: By car: From I-395 north, cross the bridge into the district and take the exit for Park Police. Turn right onto Buckeye Drive SW and then left onto Ohio Drive SW, crossing into West Potomac Park. Park anywhere along the road. Follows signs for the FDR Memorial Visitors Center to the trailhead. **Via Metro:** The nearest station is the Smithsonian; both the Blue and Orange lines travel here. It's about a 20-minute walk from there to the start of the hike. Exit the Metro on Independence Avenue and walk west. Cross 15th Street and continue straight. Cross the bridge with the tidal basin on your left and then turn left on West Basin Drive SW to the FDR Memorial Visitors Center. GPS: N38 51.542' / W77 01.404'

The Hike

Start at the Franklin Delano Roosevelt Memorial and walk through the four "rooms" representing the president's four terms in office. In the first room is a picture etched into the granite of FDR in a car on his way to his first inauguration. However, something is missing. The original photo showed him holding a long cigarette. In the second room, statues "line up" in a bread line and listen to Roosevelt's fireside chats on a radio. A statue of the thirty-second president shows him seated in his wheelchair with his beloved dog, Fala, at his feet. The memorial also has the only statue of a First Lady, Eleanor Roosevelt.

At the end of the memorial, walk out to the Tidal Basin. In spring, hundreds of cherry blossoms, a gift to the city from Japan, are in pale pink bloom all around the basin. Cross the small bridge and walk down the steps leading to the river walk. You will pass under the 14th Street Bridge and then head straight out onto the peninsula that separates the Potomac River and the Washington Channel. Across the river is the Virginia shoreline. Directly across is Ronald Reagan Washington National Airport, actually in Virginia. Planes land here every minute, using the river as an approach to the runway.

Follow the walk to Hains Point, a popular picnic and recreation spot. Continue around the point and walk on the other side of the peninsula along the Washington Channel. Boats headed for the Capital Yacht Club and the Maine Avenue Fish Market sail up the channel. Since the first days of the city, fishing boats have been selling their catches here, and it is still popular today. There are several seafood restaurants as well as fish shops along Maine Avenue.

The East Potomac Park Golf Course is in the interior part of the peninsula. There are restrooms and drinking fountains along the way.

Crossing back under the 14th Street Bridge, bear right and stop at the George Mason Memorial, located directly across from the inlet bridge. Honoring one of the founding fathers and author of the Virginia Declaration of Rights, sometimes called the precursor to the US Bill of Rights, the memorial features a small pool, benches, and a seated statue of the patriot. Some of his writings, including those against slavery, are inscribed here.

From here, it's a short walk to the Thomas Jefferson Memorial, which sits right on the Tidal Basin. The cornerstone was laid here in 1939 by President Roosevelt, a fitting connection since his memorial is not far away. The bronze statue of the third president stands facing the White House, and the walls bear quotes from his writings, which express his principles as a statesman and philosopher. There are restrooms and a gift shop in the basement of the memorial.

Miles and Directions

0.0 Starting off from Ohio Drive, walk through the memorial and exit along the Tidal Basin, moving toward the Jefferson Memorial.

1.3 Cross the inlet bridge, staying to the right and heading down steps to the riverside path. Walk along the path to the end of the peninsula.

2.5 Arrive at Hains Point. Continue around the tip of the peninsula and then walk on the other side of the peninsula, along Washington Channel.

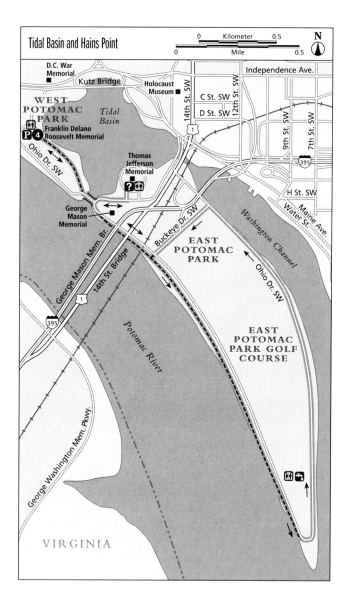

3.0 Turn left at Buckeye Drive and walk across the peninsula back to the riverside path. At the bridge, turn right and walk to the Jefferson Memorial.

4.9 Visit the Jefferson Memorial. Return to the inlet bridge and walk back into West Potomac Park.

5.4 Arrive back at West Potomac Park and the trailhead.

5 Georgetown and the Waterfront

From Roosevelt Island to Roosevelt Bridge, this hike follows the river and canal through some of the chic areas of the city. Take a break in Georgetown on the way back for a bite to eat or some shopping.

Distance: 3.8 miles out and back

Approximate hiking time: 2.5 hours

Difficulty: Easy

Trail surface: Paved; smooth dirt path along the canal

Best seasons: Year-round

Other trail users: Runners, cyclists

Canine compatibility: Leashed dogs permitted

Fees and permits: None

Schedule: Parking lot open from 6 a.m. to 10 p.m. daily

Maps: Rand McNally Washington DC Metro Street Guide: page 102; G5, F5, and G4; and page 103; A5 and A6

Finding the trailhead: By car: The parking lot at Theodore Roosevelt Island can only be accessed from the George Washington Parkway traveling north. Just after passing the Roosevelt Bridge, look for the entrance to the lot on the right. **Via Metro:** Take the Blue or the Orange line to Rosslyn. From the Rosslyn station, walk along Moore Street to 19th Street. Turn right and then left onto Lynn Street and join the hike at Lynn Street. GPS: N38 53.860' / W77 04.058'

The Hike

Leaving the tranquility of Roosevelt Island, cross over the George Washington Parkway to Rosslyn, Virginia. Now mostly hotels, offices, and high-rise apartments, this prime location across the river from Georgetown once was the home of Fort Corcoran, one of several forts protecting the capital city during the Civil War. With the housing boom that followed the Second World War, Rosslyn became a suburb of Washington, known for its garden apartments.

From Rosslyn, cross Key Bridge to Georgetown. The bridge was named for Francis Scott Key, author of the lyrics to the national anthem. Stop in the small park at the end of Key Bridge with a bust of the poet.

The C&O Canal towpath through Georgetown is a quiet respite from the busy streets above. At 31st Street, the path leads up to the road, where you can make your way down to the Washington Harbour and along the boardwalk with its beautiful view of the John F. Kennedy Center for the Performing Arts. A living memorial to JFK, this is Washington's premier performing arts center, featuring the National Symphony, opera, plays, and ballet.

As you continue along the river, you will pass the Watergate complex of hotel, offices, and posh condominiums. But it will always be most recognized as the site of the infamous Watergate scandal of 1972.

After passing under the Roosevelt Bridge, a small terrace provides views of Arlington Memorial Bridge on the left. Built in 1932, the bridge symbolizes the connection of the North and the South, with the Lincoln Memorial on the Washington, D.C. side and Arlington House, the home of Robert E. Lee, on the Virginia side. Arlington House sits on a hill in what is now Arlington Cemetery. The house belonged to Lee and his wife, Mary Custis, great-granddaughter of Martha Washington. They lived there until the outbreak of the Civil War, when the family moved to Richmond. When taxes were due on the property, Mary Custis Lee was unable to travel to Washington to pay them as it meant crossing enemy lines, and the property was repossessed by the government. When land was needed to bury those fallen at the Second Battle of Manassas, Montgomery Meigs, a classmate of Lee's at West Point, decided to use his property to create a cemetery, a way of getting back at Lee for leading the Confederate Army. After the war was over, the Lees' son fought the decision and won, but the land had become a cemetery and the family did not return. Ironically, Meigs is interred at Arlington Cemetery; Lee is not.

The three spires in the distance are the top of the US Air Force Memorial, located near the Pentagon.

Return via the same route. Or, perhaps instead of the canal towpath, you might want to walk up to M Street and window shop or stop for a bite to eat in Georgetown before heading back across the river.

Miles and Directions

0.0 Park at the Theodore Roosevelt Island parking lot. On the north side of the lot, you will see a ramp leading up to a bridge that crosses the George Washington Parkway.

0.2 After crossing the parkway, follow the path to the corner of Lynn Street. Turn right and follow the sidewalk to Key Bridge and cross using the pedestrian walkway. Follow the bridge all the way, taking care when crossing the entrance to Whitehurst Freeway.

0.6 Turn right at the Francis Scott Key Memorial Garden at the corner of Key Bridge and M Street. There is a drinking fountain here. Follow the path down to the C&O Canal towpath and turn left.

1.0 At 31st Street and the towpath, turn right down the hill, crossing K Street, and then turn left to the Washington Harbour.

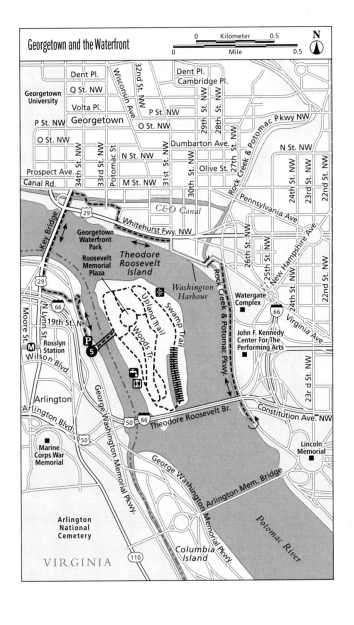

1.2 Walk along the boardwalk by the harbor.

1.3 Just past the harbor, Thompson's Boat House will be straight ahead. On the left is a short bridge leading to a parking lot. Cross that bridge and follow the path to the right that goes along the river.

1.9 Walk under Roosevelt Bridge and you will see a spot to enjoy views of the river. This is the turnaround point. Retrace your steps from here, taking a detour into Georgetown if you choose.

3.8 Arrive back at the trailhead in the Theodore Roosevelt Memorial parking lot.

Gardens and Nature

6 National Arboretum: West Side

This walk through the western side of the National Arboretum is especially vibrant during spring when the azaleas and daffodils are in bloom.

Distance: 2.1-mile loop, with an out-and-back spur to the summit of Mount Hamilton
Approximate hiking time: 2 hours
Difficulty: Moderate due to the climb up to Mount Hamilton
Trail surface: Mostly paved, some natural surfaces
Best seasons: Year-round
Other trail users: Cyclists, cars, and tour tram on paved portions
Canine compatibility: Leashed dogs permitted

Fees and permits: None
Schedule: Daily from 8 a.m. to 5 p.m.; closed Dec. 25
Maps: A walking map can be found at www.usna.usda.gov/ Information/arbormap.html. Maps are also available at the visitor center.
Trail contact: United States National Arboretum, 3501 New York Ave. NE, Washington, D.C. 20002-1958; (202) 245-2726; www.usna.usda.gov/

Finding the trailhead: By car: Take Constitution Avenue east past the Capitol Building. At Maryland Avenue, bear left and follow this to Bladensburg Road. Drive about 1 mile to R Street and turn right. The entrance gates are about 2 blocks ahead. Park in the main lot just inside the gates and near the visitor center. **Via Metro:** Take the Blue or Orange line to Stadium-Armory. From here, take the B2 bus and get off at Bladensburg Road and Rand Place. Walk 1 block back to R Street, turn left, and walk 2 blocks to the entrance gate. GPS: N38 54.727 / W76 58.184

The Hike

Walk through the visitor center to the large patio that leads out to the gardens, all of which are well-marked. Visit the National Bonsai & Penjing Museum on your left. On display here are bonsai trees and plants placed in four peaceful courtyards. This is a nice quiet place to begin or end your hike. From here, head out onto Meadow Road and into the Herb Garden.

The Herb Garden contains herbs used for culinary, medicinal, and other common purposes, as well as herbs used for industrial, spiritual, and artistic uses. These are displayed in sections by the way in which they are used and by their cultural significance—for example, those used by Native Americans. In fall, the many varieties of peppers provide a colorful display. The garden is designed in a circular shape with benches for resting and enjoying the fragrance.

From this garden, you get your first views of the National Capitol Columns across the meadow. This large meadow was created because budget cuts in the 1990s prevented management of this area. Since then, it has become an open space to allow native grasses and plants to grow and is only fully mowed once a year to promote new growth. Pathways are kept mowed to encourage visitors to explore the meadow.

Leave the Herb Garden and continue along Meadow Road to the path leading up to Mount Hamilton. As you climb, look for deer and foxes. From the 236-foot summit of the mountain, you can see as far as the US Capitol building on a clear day.

Return from the summit via the same path, then go right and immediately left into the entrance to the Boxwood and

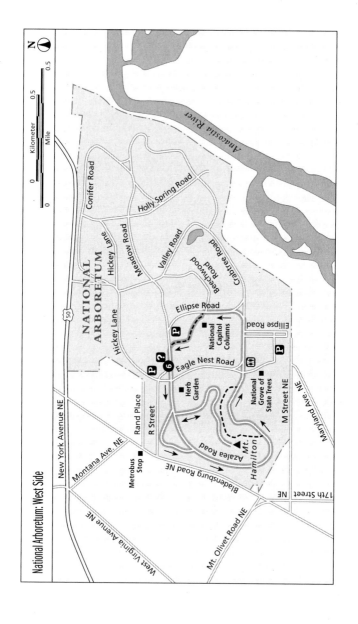

National Arboretum: West Side

Perennial Collections. About 150 varieties of boxwood can be found here. This garden is especially beautiful in winter when the bushes are bright green, and in spring when the boxwoods bloom. Boxwoods are primarily used for framing gardens, and here they frame the arboretum's Perennial Collection, which includes spring-blooming daffodils and peonies and summer-blooming daylilies.

As you exit the National Boxwood Collection, turn right and walk down Meadow Road, which changes name to Azalea Road when it curves to the left. The Azalea Collection is most spectacular in spring when thousands of bushes explode into vibrant colors. If they are not in bloom, the walk is still nice as it gets into the woods and has information along the way about azaleas.

Thanks to Washington, D.C.'s temperate climate, it was possible for most of the fifty state trees to be planted here in the National Grove of State Trees. Only a few (Alaska, Arizona, Florida, Hawaii, and South Carolina) are not included. However, "substitute" trees from each state are presented. Each tree is marked with a plaque naming the state that it represents. There are restrooms and a picnic area here as well.

The original columns that held up the dome of the US Capitol have found their final home at the arboretum. When the Capitol was being built, the dome was larger than anticipated, creating an illusion that the columns on the east side could not support the dome. While this was not the case, in 1958, the columns were taken away and replaced with larger ones that stand today. The original columns were put in storage. In 1984, the Friends of the National Arboretum raised the money to bring the columns here. Russell Page, a prominent landscape architect, designed the pool and fountain area that surrounds the columns. Today, the columns that once stood over presidential inaugurations provide a grand frame for the meadow and a relaxing spot to view the gardens.

The path that winds along the meadow leads back to the Herb Garden. Nearby is the small Friendship Garden. The plants here are easy to maintain and look like what one might find in a residential garden. The Arbor House Gift Shop in the garden sells books, cards, gardening utensils, and snacks. There are also restrooms here.

Miles and Directions

0.0 Begin at the visitor center. From the patio on the outside, walk to the far right corner and turn right onto Meadow Road. Turn right and then left into the Herb Garden.

0.1 Leave the Herb Garden and continue on Meadow Road to a parking lot on your left. Turn left and follow the path up to Mount Hamilton.

0.5 From the summit of Mount Hamilton, retrace your steps to Meadow Road. Turn right and then left into the entrance to the Perennial and Boxwood Collections.

0.7 Rejoin the road and follow it to the parking lot for the Azalea Collection, which will be on your right.

1.2 From this parking lot, walk off the road into the Azalea Collection. Follow the walking path through the collection to where it exits farther down Meadow Road.

1.5 Turn left and follow Meadow Road, crossing Eagle Nest Road, to the National Grove of State Trees on your right. There are restrooms here.

1.7 From the state trees, continue on Meadow Road. Turn left on Ellipse Road and stop at the National Capitol Columns overview.

1.8 Follow the path through the meadow to Meadow Road and turn left to the Friendship Garden next to the parking lot.

2.1 Arrive back at the trailhead and the parking lot.

7 National Arboretum: East Side

The eastern side of the National Arboretum features an Asian collection, conifers, and dogwoods. In summer, pink and white crape myrtles are in full flower, and winter brings the bright red berries of holly plants.

Distance: 2.7-mile loop
Approximate hiking time: 3 hours
Difficulty: Moderate, some hills
Trail surface: Paved and natural surfaces
Best seasons: Year-round
Other trail users: Cyclists, cars, and tour tram on paved portions
Canine compatibility: Leashed dogs permitted
Fees and permits: None

Schedule: Daily from 8 a.m. to 5 p.m.; closed Dec 25
Maps: A walking map can be found at www.usna.usda.gov/Information/arbormap.html. Maps are also available at the visitor center.
Trail contact: United States National Arboretum, 3501 New York Ave. NE, Washington, D.C. 20002-1958; (202) 245-2726; www.usna.usda.gov/

Finding the trailhead: By car: Take Constitution Avenue east past the Capitol Building. At Maryland Avenue, bear left and follow this to Bladensburg Road. Drive about 1 mile to R Street and turn right. The entrance gates will be about 2 blocks ahead. Park in the main lot just inside the gates and near the visitor center. **Via Metro:** Take the Blue or Orange line to Stadium-Armory. From here take the B2 bus and get off at Bladensburg Road and Rand Place. Walk 1 block back to R Street, turn left and walk 2 blocks to the entrance gate. GPS: N38 54.727 / W76 58.184

The Hike

The National Arboretum has many gardens and walking paths. All are well-signed and easily followed. For this hike, start with a nice wooded walk from the visitor center past several of the arboretum's research fields. After that, the Gotelli Dwarf and Slow-Growing Conifer Collection is a fascinating place to visit. There is no specific path, but you may wander through the trees as long as you wish. Most of these trees are about fifty years old, but because they are slow growing, they are very small. Look for the Hinoki false cypress, which is less than a foot tall. The collection contains other kinds of conifers as well—tall, thin junipers, weeping cedars, and pine trees. In summer, the crape myrtles add a touch of pink and white to the landscape.

Near here is the Dogwood Collection; take the short connector road to the parking area and walk into the grove toward the fountain at the far end. The state flower and tree of Virginia, dogwoods bloom in white and pink in the spring. The collection sits on a bluff overlooking the Anacostia River and is a peaceful spot any time of the year.

The Asian Collections area is a wooded hillside that stretches from the road down to the river, with several trails that meander through different sections. Something is always blooming here: If you come in the fall, amazing camellias are in bloom, and in winter, the Japanese apricot trees. Begin at the parking area that leads down through the Japanese Woodland. Most of these plants were collected in Japan and now grow successfully here, including white and yellow chrysanthemum and purple asters. Heading back up the slope, bear left and enter Asian Valley. A round patio is a nice place to rest and look straight into the valley, providing beautiful views of the collections and the Anacostia River. From the patio, continue down the hill to the red pagoda. Take the short stone trail to the right of the pagoda and walk down the slope to the river. Return back up the hill and continue past the pagoda into China Valley. In the fall, look for the dark red colors of the seven son flower tree. This trail leads back to Hickey Hill Road.

Hollies are perhaps best known for the red berries that appear in winter, giving this area a splash of color in the cold, gray weather. Magnolias are evergreens as well, so the garden is green throughout the year, with white blossoms appearing in late spring on the magnolia bushes. The arboretum has created several hybrids, including the Galaxy magnolia tree, which blooms after the last frost of spring, and the sparkleberry holly, which has red berries that last longer than other holly plants. The Holly and Magnolia Collections offer color throughout the year.

The Fern Valley Native Plant Collection displays plants native to this region—by "native," it is meant only that these plants grew here before colonization. The walk through this garden is like a miniwalk through the mid-Atlantic region, with diverse plants providing a continually changing landscape. Wetland plants grow along a small pond in the center of the collection.

If you haven't stopped at the National Capitol Columns on a hike through the west side of the arboretum, you should stop at this spot on your way back through the meadow to the trailhead and parking lot.

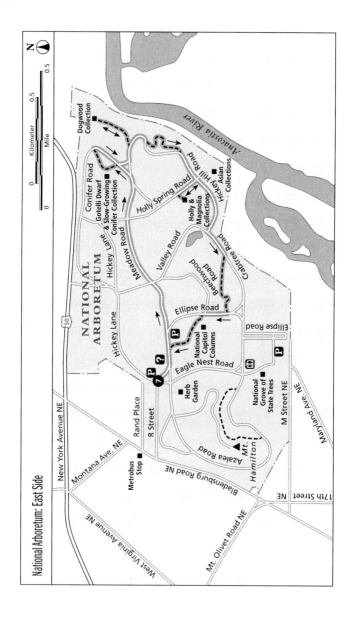

National Arboretum: East Side

Miles and Directions

0.0   Begin at the parking lot to the visitor center. Turn left on Meadow Road and cross Valley Road and Holly Spring Road.

0.7   Bear left at the fork toward Conifer Road.

0.9   Visit the slow-growing conifer collection on your left. Then return and bear left onto Hickey Hill Road. Visit the Dogwood Collection.

1.1   Follow Hickey Hill Road to the entrance to the Asian Collections. There are restrooms here, near the parking lot.

1.4   Exit the Asian Collections at China Valley and continue on Hickey Hill Road. Turn right on Holly Spring Road and see the Holly and Magnolia Collections on your left.

2.1   Return to Hickey Hill Road and turn right. The entrance to Fern Valley is on your right. Walk through this display, exiting on Ellipse Road.

2.4   Stop at the National Capitol Columns overlook if you wish.

2.7   Turn left on Meadow Road back to the trailhead and parking lot.

8 Kenilworth Aquatic Gardens

This is a short hike but well worth the time to see the amazing water flowers and plants that grow in this marsh. The trail winds around several ponds and out to the marsh that joins the Anacostia River.

Distance: 2.1 miles in two out-and-back trail sections
Approximate hiking time: 2 hours
Difficulty: Easy
Trail surface: Smooth natural paths
Best seasons: Year-round
Other trail users: None
Canine compatibility: Leashed dogs permitted
Fees and permits: None

Schedule: Daily from 7 a.m. to 4 p.m.; closed Jan 1, Thanksgiving Day, and Dec 25
Maps: A National Park Service map at www.nps.gov/keaq/planyourvisit/maps.htm. Maps are also available at the visitor center.
Trail contact: 1900 Anacostia Dr. SE, Washington, D.C. 20020; (202) 426-6905; www.nps.gov/keaq

Finding the trailhead: From I-495, take the exit for US 50 west (exit 19B). Merge onto MD 295 south and take the exit for Eastern Avenue/Aquatic Gardens. Stay straight onto Kenilworth Avenue. Turn right on Quarles Street, and then left on Anacostia Avenue. Park in the lot by the road and walk into the park to the visitor center. GPS: N38 54.76 / W76 56.516

The Hike

What began as a pond with a few water lilies in William Shaw's backyard in the 1880s has blossomed into Kenilworth Aquatic Gardens. Set along the Anacostia River, in an area called the Kenilworth Marsh, the gardens contain an array of ponds with thousands of blooming water flowers, including several varieties of water lilies. These bloom in the late spring and summer and are best during the morning before temperatures get too hot—they tend to close up if it reaches over 90 degrees.

The park is popular with birders, who look for rails, sparrows, and blackbirds. Ducks and Canada geese are very abundant and easy to spot. Several types of wildlife also reside in the park including frogs, turtles, muskrats, and beavers; and butterflies and dragonflies buzz around the marsh pools.

Boardwalks lead out to the mudflats right along the river. Look for great blue herons and other water birds as you walk out there. On the Marsh and River Trail, walk between the Kenilworth Marsh and a wooded swamp to the end, where the two meet the Anacostia River. Many people visit the area by canoe, so you might see some on the river. A seawall was built here in the early twentieth century; remnants can be seen today along the river's edge. Unfortunately, the seawall proved to be ecologically unfriendly and didn't prevent flooding as it was intended.

Kenilworth is the only national park dedicated to water plants. The visitor center has restrooms and sells bottled water and gifts. The park rangers are very helpful and can answer most of your questions.

Miles and Directions

0.0 Start at the visitor center.

0.2 Go left and out into the lily pond area.

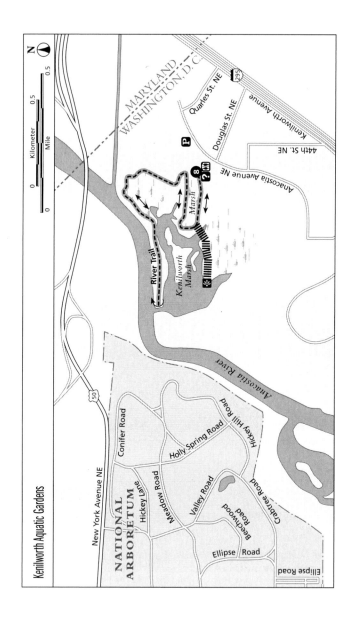

Kenilworth Aquatic Gardens

0.3 Go straight onto the boardwalk out to the mudflats.

0.5 Return from the mudflat viewing area and head left along the other side of the lilies.

0.7 As you approach the visitor center head left and join the Marsh and River Trail.

1.4 Come to the end of the trail. Retrace your steps toward the visitor center.

2.1 Arrive back at the trailhead and visitor center.

9 Rock Creek Park: Historical Loop

This short hike takes you away from the city and features three historic sites: Fort DeRussy, Miller Cabin, and Milkhouse Ford.

Distance: 1.8-mile lollipop

Approximate hiking time: 1.5 hours

Difficulty: Easy

Trail surface: Natural and paved surfaces

Best seasons: Year-round

Other trail users: Runners, horses

Canine compatibility: Leashed dogs permitted

Fees and permits: None

Schedule: Always open; nature center open Wed through Sun from 9 a.m. to 5 p.m.

Maps: National Park Service maps at www.nps.gov/rocr; trail maps available at the nature center

Trail contact: Rock Creek Park, 3545 Williamsburg Lane NW, Washington, D.C. 20008; (202) 895-6000; www.nps.gov/rocr

Finding the trailhead: By car: On I-66, cross the Roosevelt Bridge. At the end of the bridge, take the right-hand exit for Independence Avenue. At the T intersection, bear right and then bear right again onto unsigned Independence Avenue toward the Kennedy Center. Follow the signs for Beach Drive. Beach Drive winds through the park for about two miles; continue to follow Beach Drive until you see signs for the nature center. Follow these signs, which will take you onto Ridge Road and to Glover Road, toward the entrance to the nature center. Park at the nature center. **Via Metro:** Take the Red line to the Van Ness–UDC station and exit onto Connecticut Avenue. Beginning the 1.2-mile walk to the trailhead, head north on Connecticut Avenue and turn right on Davenport Street. Follow this street into Rock Creek Park, where it becomes Grant Road. Turn right onto

Ridge Road, then left onto Glover Road. Then make another left into the nature center. GPS: N38 57.561' / W77 03.103'

The Hike

One of the oldest national parks, Rock Creek Park was designed to create an outdoor haven for city dwellers. Its 1,752 acres include hiking trails, bike trails, a golf course, a tennis center, horse stables and equestrian trails, historic sites, and outdoor entertainment venues. Carter Barron Amphitheater was built in 1950 as part of the celebration of the 150th anniversary of the capital city. Performances held at the outdoor theater throughout the summer include musicals, plays, and concerts. Among the historic sites that can be visited is Peirce Mill, one of a series of gristmills built along the creek and the only one left today. The jurisdiction of Rock Creek Park extends into Georgetown and includes the Old Stone House at 3051 M St. NW; this is the oldest house in the district, dating back to 1760.

The trail begins at the nature center. After crossing Military Road, the trail leads east to Fort DeRussy. Built in 1861 to defend Washington during the Civil War, it was part of a system of twelve forts built as a defense around the city. All that remains today are earthen mounds and remnants of the trenches.

From the fort, the trail continues southeast and then winds north to parallel the creek and reach the Miller Cabin.

The Miller Cabin was built in 1863 by the poet Joaquin Miller. This colorful character moved to Washington from the West, but soon discovered that he didn't like city life and chose to live here so he could better connect with his muse. He lived here for a couple of years before returning to California. The site is now used for the Miller Cabin Poetry

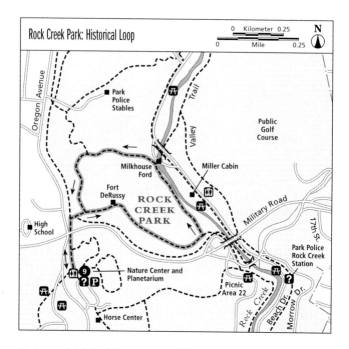

Rock Creek Park: Historical Loop

Series, which holds poetry readings every Tuesday evening in June and July.

The hike continues north to Milkhouse Ford, an old vehicle crossing point. From here the trail heads west again, and then south back to the nature center. There is more information at the center, as well as a small planetarium. The park offers many programs throughout the year, including ranger-led walks and horse rides, stargazing evenings, and bird-watching tours.

Miles and Directions

0.0 Start at the nature center. Walk down the bike path heading north and cross Military Road.

0.3 Follow the trail to the right and arrive at Fort DeRussy. Continue southeast to the creek.

0.7 The trail bears left and goes north along the left side of the creek to Miller Cabin.

1.1 At Milkhouse Ford, the trail bears left again and then south as it winds back down to Military Road.

1.8 Return to the trailhead and nature center parking lot.

10 Rock Creek Park: Rapids Bridge Loop

See the rapids of Rock Creek on this wooded hike through the park. Look for deer and foxes along the trail.

Distance: 2-mile lollipop
Approximate hiking time: 1.5 hours
Difficulty: Easy
Trail surface: Natural surfaces
Best seasons: Year-round
Other trail users: Runners, horses
Canine compatibility: Leashed dogs permitted
Fees and permits: None

Schedule: Always open; nature center open Wed through Sun from 9 a.m. to 5 p.m.
Maps: National Park Service maps at www.nps.gov/rocr; trail maps available at the nature center
Trail contact: Rock Creek Park, 3545 Williamsburg Lane NW, Washington, D.C. 20008; (202) 895-6000; www.nps.gov/rocr

Finding the trailhead: By car: On I-66, cross the Roosevelt Bridge. At the end of the bridge, take the right-hand exit for Independence Avenue. At the T intersection, bear right and then bear right again onto unsigned Independence Avenue toward the Kennedy Center. Follow the signs for Beach Drive. Beach Drive winds through the park for about two miles; continue to follow Beach Drive until you see signs for the nature center. Follow these signs, which will take you onto Ridge Road and Glover Road toward the entrance to the nature center. Park at the nature center. **Via Metro:** Take the Red line to Van Ness–UDC station. To begin the 1.2-mile walk to the nature center, exit onto Connecticut Avenue. Head north on

Connecticut and turn right on Davenport Street. Follow this street into Rock Creek Park, where it becomes Grant Road. Turn right onto Ridge Road, left onto Glover Road, and then left into the nature center. GPS: N38 57.561' / W77 03.103'

The Hike

Rock Creek Park is a true urban oasis. Right in the middle of the city, you can head into the woods on foot or horseback, see fall colors, hear nothing but birds and rushing water, and smell earthy fresh air. Washingtonians can see brilliant fall colors and early spring blossoms without leaving the city.

The horse center at Rock Creek Park offers boarding, trail rides, riding lessons, and a therapeutic riding program. President Reagan, an avid horseman, often came here to ride. You will probably see some horses around the stable as you begin this hike. Following the path from the horse center, join the trail, which takes you through woods of hardwood trees, tulip poplars, and beeches.

The portion of the creek that is to the left of the trail is one of the most scenic parts of the park. This section of the creek flows over granite boulders, once part of an ancient mountain that separated the piedmont plateau from the coastal plain. The rocks create a series of rapids, which can be best seen from Rapids Bridge. Walk across to get the best view before returning to the trail.

The trail continues uphill, under Ross Drive, and then back to the stables and the trailhead.

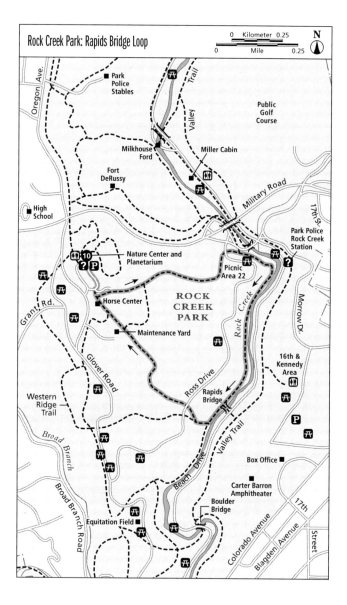

Rock Creek Park: Rapids Bridge Loop

Kilometer 0 0.25

Mile 0 0.25

N

Oregon Ave.

Park Police Stables

Valley Trail

Public Golf Course

Milkhouse Ford

Miller Cabin

Fort DeRussy

Military Road

High School

17th St.

Park Police Rock Creek Station

Nature Center and Planetarium

10

?

P

Picnic Area 22

Grant Rd.

Horse Center

ROCK CREEK PARK

Rock Creek

Morrow Dr.

Maintenance Yard

16th & Kennedy Area

Gloves Road

Ross Drive

Rapids Bridge

Western Ridge Trail

Broad Branch

Beach Drive

Valley Trail

Box Office

Carter Barron Amphitheater

Broad Branch Road

Equitation Field

Boulder Bridge

Colorado Avenue

Blagden Avenue

17th

Street

Miles and Directions

0.0 Start at the nature center parking lot. Walk down to the horse stables. Turn left at the wooden fences, which is the beginning of the trail.

0.4 At picnic area 22, follow the trail south along the creek.

1.2 Arrive at Rapids Bridge. From here, follow the trail as it turns right and back up to the horse center.

2.0 Arrive back at the trailhead and nature center parking lot.

11 Rock Creek Park: Boulder Bridge Loop

This hike is similar to Rock Creek Park's Rapids Bridge hike, but it goes a little farther and includes Boulder Bridge. Built in 1902, this scenic bridge is now on the National Register of Historic Places.

Distance: 3.0-mile loop

Approximate hiking time: 2 hours

Difficulty: Moderate

Trail surface: Natural surfaces

Best seasons: Year-round

Other trail users: Runners, horses

Canine compatibility: Leashed dogs permitted

Fees and permits: None

Schedule: Always open; nature center open Wed through Sun from 9 a.m. to 5 p.m.

Maps: National Park Service maps at www.nps.gov/rocr; trail maps available at the nature center

Trail contact: Rock Creek Park, 3545 Williamsburg Lane NW, Washington, D.C. 20008; (202) 895-6000; www.nps.gov/rocr

Finding the trailhead: By car: On I-66, cross the Roosevelt Bridge. At the end of the bridge, take the right-hand exit for Independence Avenue. At the T intersection, bear right and then bear right again onto unsigned Independence Avenue toward the Kennedy Center. Follow the signs for Beach Drive. Beach Drive winds through the park for about two miles; continue to follow Beach Drive until you see signs for the nature center. Follow these signs, which will take you onto Ridge Road and Glover Road toward the entrance to the nature center. Park at the nature center. **Via Metro:** Take the Red line to Van Ness–UDC station. To begin the 1.2-mile walk to the nature center, head north on Connecticut Avenue. Turn right onto

Davenport Street and follow it to Rock Creek Park, where it becomes Grant Road. Turn right onto Ridge Road, left onto Glover Road, and then left into the nature center. GPS: N38 57.561' / W77 03.103'

The Hike

The area that is now Rock Creek Park was inhabited for centuries by Native Americans, most recently the Nacotchtank tribe in the 1500s and 1600s. It is believed that Captain John Smith explored parts of Rock Creek on his ventures up the Potomac River. In the 1700s and 1800s, mills were built along the creek to harvest water power to mill grain and lumber. These mills were phased out after steam power proved more efficient.

The main road through the park is called Beach Drive, which could be confusing to some as there are no beaches in the park. The road was named for Lansing Beach, the director of the construction of the road.

From the nature center, walk south down a hill to the horse center, which is clearly marked. Walk around the wooden fences and bear left on the trail. When you come to picnic area 22, follow the trail along the creek and the rapids. Cross over Rapids Bridge and follow the Valley Trail (blue blazes) to the right. Mountain laurel grows along the side of the trail here. Walk down to Boulder Bridge. The best view is from the north side, before you cross the bridge, so have your cameras ready.

After crossing Boulder Bridge, take the smaller trail on the right up the hill to connect with the Western Ridge Trail (green blazes). Cross the Equitation Field, part of the horse center, and then hike back into the woods. Look for Virginia pines on this portion of the hike, before returning to the trailhead at the nature center and parking lot.

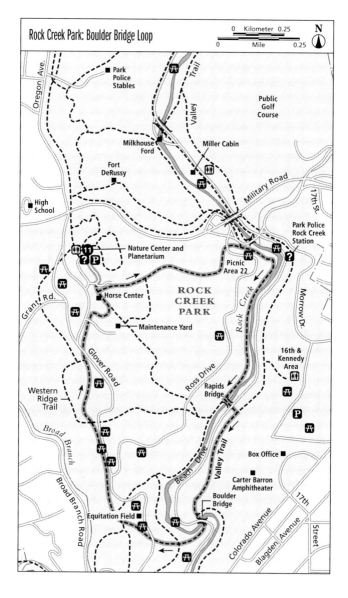

Rock Creek Park: Boulder Bridge Loop

0 Kilometer 0.25
0 Mile 0.25

N

Oregon Ave.

Park Police Stables

Valley Trail

Public Golf Course

Milkhouse Ford

Miller Cabin

Fort DeRussy

Military Road

17th St.

High School

Park Police Rock Creek Station

Nature Center and Planetarium

Picnic Area 22

Rock Creek

Morrow Dr.

Horse Center

ROCK CREEK PARK

Grant Rd.

Maintenance Yard

16th & Kennedy Area

Western Ridge Trail

Glover Road

Ross Drive

Rapids Bridge

Broad Branch

Box Office

Beach Drive

Carter Barron Amphitheater

Valley Trail

Broad Branch Road

Equitation Field

Boulder Bridge

Colorado Avenue

Blagden Avenue

17th

Street

Miles and Directions

0.0 Start at the nature center parking lot. Walk south down to the horse stables. Turn left at the wooden fences, which is the beginning of the trail.

0.4 At picnic area 22, follow the trail south along the creek.

1.2 Arrive at Rapids Bridge. Cross over and continue on the Valley Trail on the other (east) side of the creek.

1.4 Cross Boulder Bridge. Follow the connector trail to the right as it winds to the south, and then back north to the Western Ridge Trail.

1.8 Arrive at Equitation Field. Turn left into the wooded area to continue on the trail.

3.0 Arrive back at the trailhead and the nature center parking lot.

12 Glover-Archbold Park

If you're tired of being in the city, but don't have time to go out to the country, this short hike through the woods will restore your spirits and bring you back to nature.

Distance: 2.6 miles out and back

Approximate hiking time: 1.5 hours

Difficulty: Easy, but some of the trail might be rocky or muddy

Trail surface: Natural surfaces; a few stream crossings

Best seasons: Year-round

Other trail users: None

Canine compatibility: Leashed dogs permitted

Fees and permits: None

Schedule: Always open

Maps: National Park Service map at www.nps.gov/rocr; Rand McNally Washington DC Metro Street Guide: page 103; E2, E3, and E4

Trail contacts: Rock Creek Park Headquarters, 3545 Williamsburg Lane NW, 20008; (202) 895-6000; visitor information (202) 895-6070; www.nps.gov/rocr/

Finding the trailhead: From Wisconsin Avenue in Georgetown, turn left onto Reservoir Road NW. After about 0.25 mile, turn right onto 37th Street NW. After about 0.5 mile, 37th Street bears slightly left and becomes Tunlaw Road. Follow Tunlaw Road to 42nd Street, turn left on 42nd Street, and park anywhere along the road. GPS: N38 55.428' / W77 04.903'

The Hike

Glover-Archbold Park is a wooded oasis in the midst of the city. Named for two Washington citizens who donated land for the park, it is part of the larger Rock Creek Park system. Portions of the path follow Foundry Branch, which

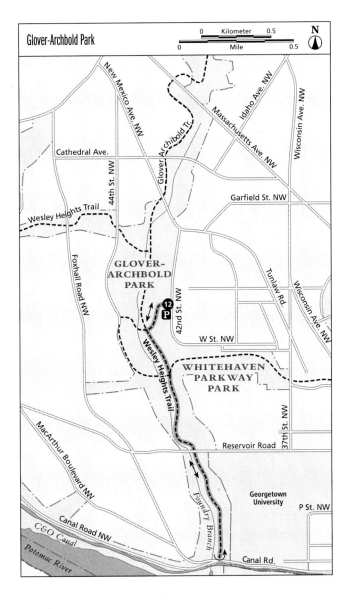

Glover-Archbold Park

Kilometer
0   0.5

Mile
0   0.5

N

New Mexico Ave. NW

Glover Archbold Tr.

Massachusetts Ave. NW

Idaho Ave. NW

Wisconsin Ave. NW

Cathedral Ave.

44th St. NW

Garfield St. NW

Wesley Heights Trail

Foxhall Road NW

GLOVER-
ARCHBOLD
PARK

Tunlaw Rd.

Wisconsin Ave. NW

12
P

42nd St. NW

W St. NW

Wesley Heights Trail

WHITEHAVEN
PARKWAY
PARK

MacArthur Boulevard NW

37th St. NW

Reservoir Road

Foundry Branch

Georgetown
University

P St. NW

Canal Road NW

C&O Canal

Canal Rd.

Potomac River

leads to the C&O Canal. Depending on the season and the precipitation, the creek can be nearly a dry bed, or can hold gently flowing water. Autumn is a wonderful time to hike here, when the old oak and beech trees turn color and the weather is crisp. In summer, it's a cool oasis from Washington's humidity.

The surrounding neighborhood is mostly residential condominiums and apartments, with a community garden at the corner of Tunlaw Street and 42nd Street. You will see many people walking their dogs through the park.

The park is popular for bird-watching; warblers and thrushes can be seen in spring and fall, and look for wrens in the winter.

The nearby neighborhood of Glover Park, along Wisconsin Avenue, offers plenty of post-hike places to eat and drink.

Miles and Directions

0.0 Begin hiking from the trailhead at the 42nd Street entrance to the park.

0.1 Join the Wesley Heights Trail and turn left, following the creek on your right.

0.5 You will see a sign on your left stating C&O Canal Trail, 1 mile. Continue straight on the Wesley Heights Trail.

0.7 Cross the creek to the right.

0.8 The Wesley Heights Trail ends at Reservoir Road. Cross the road and bear left down a sidewalk and along a dirt path across a field. Enter the woods again and follow an unmarked trail.

1.3 The trail ends at Foxhall Road. Return the way you came.

2.6 Arrive back at the trailhead on 42rd Street.

The C&O Canal

13 C&O Canal: Lock 8 to Lock 6

This smooth portion of the C&O Canal towpath follows the canal with views of a rocky branch of the Potomac River.

Distance: 6 miles out and back
Approximate hiking time: 3 hours
Difficulty: Moderate
Trail surface: Dirt, slightly stony. Short paths to the river are rocky and steep.
Best seasons: Year-round
Other trail users: Bicyclists
Canine compatibility: Leashed dogs permitted
Fees and permits: None
Schedule: Always open

Maps: Trail map at www.nps .gov/choh/planyourvisit/upload/ chohmap.pdf
Special considerations: Be mindful of cyclists; this is a popular biking trail.
Trail contact: Chesapeake & Ohio Canal National Historical Park, 1057 Thomas Jefferson St. NW, Washington, D.C. 20007; (202) 653-5190; www.nps.gov/ choh

Finding the trailhead: From I-495, take the exit for Clara Barton Parkway/Glen Echo. Follow Clara Barton Parkway south. Pass the Lock 10 parking lot on the right and then turn right into the Lock 8/ River House parking lot. GPS: N38 56.880' / W77 07.502'

The Hike

The C&O Canal National Historical Park stretches for 185 miles from Georgetown to Cumberland, Maryland. The canal provided a trade link between the Chesapeake Bay and the western frontier. The project was started in 1828, on the same day as construction began on the Baltimore & Ohio Railroad, which ran from Baltimore to Cumberland. The competition between the two methods of transportation carried on through the nineteenth century, and, after economic setbacks and two major floods, the canal was taken over by the railroad and closed in 1924. It was established as a national historic landmark in 1971, and today provides recreational and educational opportunities. The towpath parallels the canal and is a popular biking and hiking trail.

This portion of the C&O Canal National Historical Park begins at Lock House 8, also known as River House. Built in the 1830s, it was home to the lockkeeper for almost a century. After the canal was no longer used for transportation and commerce, the building fell into disrepair. Only recently has the Potomac Conservancy been able to restore the house, and it is now open for visitors on weekends, March through October. The new center hosts several special events; visit www.potomac.org/site/discover-rclh8/ for more information.

After crossing a couple of bridges, take a look at the old lock before joining the C&O Canal towpath. Shortly after you turn left onto the towpath, you will see several small trails on the right leading to a branch of the Potomac River. Take any of these trails if you wish to get a nice view of the rocks in the Potomac, south of Great Falls. You can also see the American Legion Bridge in the distance, which connects Virginia and Maryland via the Capitol Beltway (I-495). Some of the side trails are a bit steep, so be careful—but none are very long.

Follow the path to Lock 7, where a similar lockkeeper's house stands along with the ruins of the lock. Continue on the path to Lock 6. (*Note:* The lockkeeper's house here has been renovated and is available for overnight stays. Visit www.canalquarters.org/lockhouse-6.php for more information.)

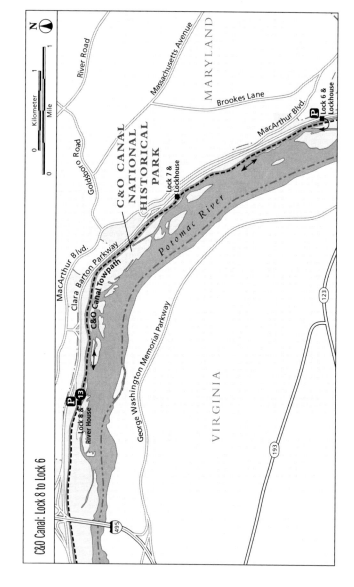

C&O Canal: Lock 8 to Lock 6

On the way to Lock 6, you will pass Little Falls; this was the site where President John Quincy Adams broke ground for the canal on July 4, 1828. There is a pumping station here and ruins of a small dam.

The path follows straight along the canal and is shady in the summertime. If the water level is low, it could be buggy, so be sure to have some repellent. It can get muddy after a heavy rain. Fall colors are spectacular.

When you reach Lock 6, turn around and retrace your steps back to the trailhead.

Miles and Directions

0.0 Start on the trail leading from the parking lot down to the canal and the River House. Cross the two small wooden bridges to join the C&O Canal towpath and turn left. Follow the trail toward Lock 7.

1.4 Continue straight as you pass Lock 7. You'll see an old lock house on the left.

3.0 At Lock 6, turn around and return the same route.

6.0 Return to the trailhead at Lock 8.

14 C&O Canal: Lock 6 to Fletchers Cove

This shady trail follows the C&O Canal towpath along the canal to Fletchers Cove on the Potomac River. Stop along the way to cross Chain Bridge to Virginia, where you will enjoy nice views of Little Great Falls, the lower portion of Great Falls.

Distance: 4.3 miles out and back

Approximate hiking time: 2.5 hours

Difficulty: Moderate

Trail surface: Smooth, but a little stony in places; can be a little muddy after it rains

Best seasons: Year-round

Other trail users: Cyclists, runners

Canine compatibility: Leashed dogs permitted

Fees and permits: None

Schedule: Always open

Maps: Trail map at www.nps .gov/choh/planyourvisit/upload/ chohmap.pdf

Trail contact: Chesapeake & Ohio Canal National Historical Park, 1057 Thomas Jefferson St. NW, Washington, D.C. 20007; (202) 653-5190; www.nps.gov/ choh

Finding the trailhead: From I-495, take the exit for Clara Barton Parkway/Glen Echo. Follow Clara Barton Parkway south. You will pass the Lock 10 and Lock 8 parking lots on the right, and then turn right into the Lock 6 parking lot. GPS: N38 58.252' / W77 09.675'

The Hike

This part of the C&O Canal towpath starts at Lock 6. The lockkeeper's house here is available for overnight rental;

visit www.canalquarters.org/lockhouse-6.php for information. Cross the lock via a small bridge and turn left onto the towpath. The path here is mostly forested on the right; in winter you catch glimpses of the Potomac River.

At Lock 5, as you bear right to stay on the path, you will cross an inlet lock. When the canal was in use, if the water level got low, a gate could be opened to allow water from the river to flow into the canal. You will notice the canal has a much higher water level from this point on, and the possibility of seeing waterfowl, mostly ducks, is greater. You will cross from Maryland into the District of Columbia after passing Lock 5.

The first Chain Bridge was constructed in 1797 and was made of chain trusses, hence the name. This bridge collapsed in the 1850s and, subsequently, seven more bridges have been built at this crossing. The present bridge is made of steel, but has kept the historical name of Chain Bridge. It connects Washington with Fairfax County, Virginia.

The views from the center of Chain Bridge are of the Little Great Falls. This rocky portion of the river is popular with experienced kayakers, but is quite dangerous. Walk almost all the way across the bridge for the best views, then return to the towpath and continue south toward Fletchers Cove.

On the way to Fletchers Cove, you will pass under an old railroad trestle that is part of the Capital Crescent Trail—a very busy bike trail that connects Georgetown to Silver Spring, Maryland. Notice the charming old lanterns hanging from the top of the bridge. On weekdays, the trail is very crowded with bike commuters, and on weekends with recreational cyclists.

Fletchers Cove is a great place to break your hike with a picnic, or even a paddle in a rowboat or canoe. The area

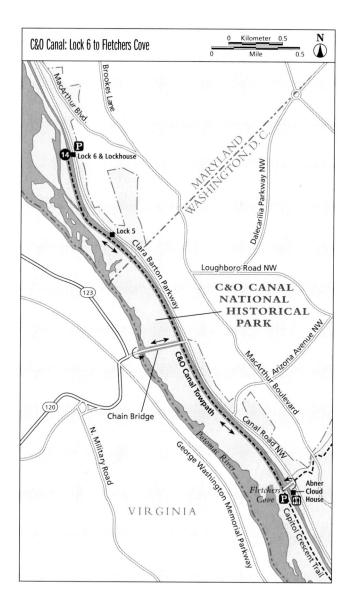

C&O Canal: Lock 6 to Fletchers Cove

0   Kilometer   0.5

0   Mile   0.5

N

MacArthur Blvd.

Brookes Lane

P
14 Lock 6 & Lockhouse

MARYLAND

WASHINGTON, D.C.

Lock 5

Clara Barton Parkway

Loughboro Road NW

Dalecarilia Parkway NW

C&O CANAL
NATIONAL
HISTORICAL
PARK

Arizona Avenue NW

MacArthur Boulevard

123

C&O Canal Towpath

Canal Road NW

Chain Bridge

120

N Military Road

Potomac River

George Washington Memorial Parkway

VIRGINIA

Fletchers
Cove

P

Abner
Cloud
House

Capitol Crescent Trail

is renowned for great fishing. Fletchers Boathouse has operated here since the 1850s and is open spring, summer, and fall; visit www.fletcherscove.com for more information. Boats are only allowed to travel south of the cove—not near the falls. Snacks are available.

Before heading back on the towpath, take a short walk up to the Abner Cloud House, the oldest remaining building on the canal. It was built by Abner Cloud, who ran a grain mill that provided flour to Washington from 1802 to 1870. The house is now owned by the National Society of the Colonial Dames of America and is not open to visitors.

Miles and Directions

0.0 Start in the parking lot for Lock 6. Follow the trail around the lockhouse and cross two small bridges.

0.2 Turn left onto the C&O Canal towpath.

0.5 Arrive at Lock 5. Cross the bridge on the left for restrooms on the left and a drinking fountain on the right. Cross back over the bridge and bear left to cross the bridge to continue on the path. Follow the path to Chain Bridge.

0.7 Arrive at Chain Bridge. There will be a ramp to go up to the bridge and a pedestrian walkway. Walk across the bridge for views of the Potomac River and the lower part of Great Falls.

1.0 Return to the towpath.

1.3 Rejoin the towpath. Follow this to Fletchers Cove.

2.3 Return the same way from Fletchers Cove—remaining on the towpath instead of crossing Chain Bridge again.

4.3 Arrive back at the trailhead at Lock 6.

Just Outside
the District

15 Fort Washington

On the site of the ruins of a fort built to protect Washington, D.C., during the War of 1812, Fort Washington has served as a protective barrier for the city since the Civil War. Today it is a park with a rich history that sits on the banks of the Potomac River in Maryland, just outside the District.

Distance: 2.9 miles out and back, with a short loop through Fort Washington
Approximate hiking time: 3 hours, including time to visit the fort
Difficulty: Easy
Trail surface: Paved and natural surfaces
Best seasons: Year-round
Other trail users: None
Canine compatibility: Leashed dogs permitted
Fees and permits: A small fee per car

Schedule: Daily from 8 a.m. to sunset; visitor center and fort open 9 a.m. to 5 p.m.; closed Jan 1, Thanksgiving Day, and Dec 25
Maps: A National Park Service map is at www.nps.gov/fowa. Maps are also available at the entrance gate and the visitor center.
Trail contact: Fort Washington Park, 13551 Fort Washington Rd., Fort Washington, MD 20744; (301) 763-4600; www.nps.gov/fowa

Finding the trailhead: From I-95/495 take exit 3, for the Indian Head Highway south/MD 210. Travel about 4 miles to Fort Washington Road and turn right. The park is located at the end of the road. After passing through the entrance gate, follow signs to the visitor center. GPS: N38 42.789' W77 01.887'

The Hike

This prime location on the river just south of Washington, D.C., was originally the site of Fort Warburton, built to protect the capital city. However, in 1814, during the War of 1812, the British were able to invade Washington anyway, and Fort Warburton was destroyed by Americans so that it wouldn't fall into British hands.

Shortly after the war ended, reconstruction began and Fort Washington was established in the 1840s. During the Civil War, with Confederate Virginia just across the river, it served to protect Washington from the South. Just before World War II, the fort closed and was turned over to the Director of Public Buildings. With the entry of the United States into the war, the fort reopened temporarily as the Adjutant General School, and was returned to the Department of the Interior. It's now a national park rich in history and popular for hiking and family picnics.

As you walk from the parking lot to the visitor center, you will pass the ruins of Battery Decatur. This structure once held two cannons on the top, with ammunition and gunpowder stored below. The visitor center has maps and books on the history if you want to explore further. Spend some time at the fort going through the barracks, kitchen, and up to the rows of cannons along the wall. There are nice views of the river from the end of the fort.

The Potomac River was, and still is, an important route for commerce. The river presents navigational issues with its rocks and other hazards. The Fort Washington lighthouse was not officially part of the fort, but when it was decided a lighthouse was necessary, the first one was built in 1857 and

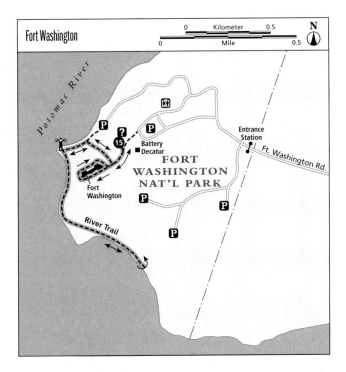

became the responsibility of the ordnance sergeant. It was originally a simple pole with a light on top. It evolved into a tower with reflecting lamp on top, a light keeper's house, boathouse, and a dock. There is still a beacon here, operated by the US Coast Guard, but the lighthouse itself has been out of commission since 1954.

From the lighthouse, pick up the River Trail. Walking along the river, look for waterfowl and beavers along the water's edge. At the battery ruins, turn around. Retrace your steps along the River Trail to return to the fort and trailhead.

Miles and Directions

0.0 Begin at the visitor center parking lot. Follow the path past the ruins on the right.

0.1 Stop at the visitor center for information and a map. There are restrooms here as well.

0.2 Follow the path to the entrance to the fort.

0.3 Walk around the various parts of the fort. After your tour, go back through the entrance and turn left onto the path toward the lighthouse.

0.5 Arrive at the lighthouse, then retrace your steps back to the main path.

0.7 Back on the main path, turn right to follow the River Trail.

1.0 Cross a wooden bridge. Continue on the trail.

1.8 Arrive at the ruins of a small battery. Return the way you came.

2.9 Arrive back at the trailhead and visitor center.

16 Great Falls Park

Just north of Washington, D.C., the Great Falls cascade over rocks in the Potomac River. This hike, on the Virginia side, winds along the cliffs over the river and then past remnants of the Patowmack Canal.

Distance: 2.7-mile loop
Approximate hiking time: 2.5 hours
Difficulty: Easy
Trail surface: Natural surfaces
Best seasons: Year-round
Other trail users: Cyclists on some portions
Canine compatibility: Leashed dogs permitted
Fees and permits: A small fee per car
Schedule: Daily from 7 a.m. to dusk; closed Dec 25

Maps: A National Park Service map is available at www.nps .gov/grfa; maps are also available at the entrance gate and the visitor center.
Special considerations: There is no swimming allowed. This part of the river is very dangerous.
Trail contact: Great Falls Park, c/o Turkey Run Park, George Washington Memorial Parkway, McLean, VA 22101; (703) 285-2965; www.nps.gov/grfa

Finding the trailhead: From the Capital Beltway (I-495), take exit 44 for Route 193/Georgetown Pike. Follow this for about 3 miles and turn right onto Old Dominion Drive at the sign for the park entrance. Follow Old Dominion Drive for about a mile to the park gate, then continue to the parking lot. GPS: N38 59.862' / W77 15.333'

The Hike

Stop first at the visitor center, which has information on the falls, hiking trail maps, and a short video on the history of the town and canal that were once here.

Great Falls is created where the Potomac River meets a series of rocks and Mather Gorge, named for the first director of the National Park Service. This spectacular sight is popular year-round. The three overlooks just off the picnic area are easy to get to—the third one offers the best views and is the most accessible.

Across from Overlook 3 is a high-water marker that shows, unbelievably, how high the river has flooded over the years. Because the gorge is so narrow, any extreme amounts of water, from hurricanes or excessive snowmelt, cause the river to rise several feet over the cliffs. In March 2010, the melt from an unusually snowy winter brought the river level right to the top of the cliffs.

This loop through the park is described in a clockwise direction. As you continue along the River Trail, the path narrows and there is a small area where you will need to climb over some rocks. Stop along the way and go to the cliff edge for more great views. The river is a bit calmer here, and you will likely see kayakers in the water. Swimming is forbidden as the water is very rough. This area is also popular with rock climbers and, on a nice day, you will likely encounter climbing groups as you make your way along the river.

The Matildaville Trail takes you through the ruins of what once was a thriving town. George Washington surveyed this land when he was young and had the idea to bypass this rough part of the river by building a system of canals around it to create a trade route between Virginia and the Ohio Valley. The Patowmack Canal, a precursor to the C&O Canal, was completed in 1802 and brought goods from Cumberland, Maryland, to the Washington area for almost thirty years. The town of Matildaville was established in 1790 by "Lighthorse Harry" Lee, and was situated on the canal. It fell into decline in the 1820s after the canal ceased to operate. On the Matildaville Trail, faint remains of the city can be seen.

Heading back toward the trailhead on the Old Carriage Road, you walk along the ruins of the canal and its locks. The canal was bought by the C&O Canal Company, which went on to build a continuous canal on the other side of the river.

In the early twentieth century, a railroad was built from Georgetown through parts of northern Virginia and culminated at Great Falls, where there was an amusement park, dance hall, and restaurant. An evening of dinner and dancing was often topped off by a romantic walk by the falls.

Returning to the visitor center, you will walk through the large park area, popular for family picnics.

Miles and Directions

0.0 From the parking lot, head toward the visitor center. Restrooms, snacks, and drinking water are available here. Continue to the beginning of the path leading to the falls overlooks. There are three signed overlooks, and all have tremendous views.

0.3 After visiting Overlook 3 and returning to the main path, turn left to follow the River Trail.

0.5 To continue on the River Trail, go down the steps and across the small bridge.

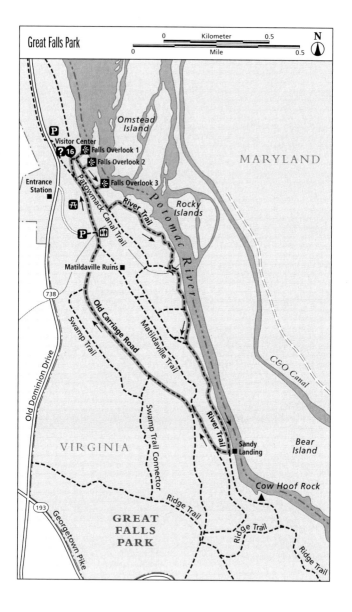

Great Falls Park

Kilometer
0   0.5
Mile
0   0.5

N

MARYLAND

Omstead Island

Visitor Center

Falls Overlook 1

Falls Overlook 2

Falls Overlook 3

Entrance Station

Potowmack Canal Trail

River Trail

Rocky Islands

P o t o m a c   R i v e r

Matildaville Ruins

Old Carriage Road

Swamp Trail

Matildaville Trail

C&O Canal

Old Dominion Drive

738

Swamp Trail Connector

River Trail

Sandy Landing

Bear Island

Cow Hoof Rock

VIRGINIA

Ridge Trail

Ridge Trail

Ridge Trail

GREAT FALLS PARK

193

Georgetown Pike

0.7 Follow signs to stay on the River Trail; you will turn left and then turn right.

1.1 Come to a road that leads left down to Sandy Landing, a launching area for boats. Turn right and follow the signs for the Matildaville Trail.

1.5 Join the Old Carriage Road; turn right.

2.1 Cross a large meadow, and then turn left and right to stay on the Old Carriage Road.

2.5 Turn left toward the visitor center. There are restrooms and a drinking fountain here.

2.7 Return to the trailhead and visitor center.

17 Mason Neck State Park: Beach and Bay

This short hike features the water and marshes of the Mason Neck area. Look for ducks, swans, and geese, especially in spring and fall.

Distance: 2.6-mile double loop
Approximate hiking time: 2.5 hours
Difficulty: Easy
Trail surface: Natural surfaces, boardwalks, and pavement
Best seasons: Year-round
Other trail users: None
Canine compatibility: Leashed dogs permitted
Fees and permits: A small fee per car on weekdays; the fee is slightly higher on weekends

Schedule: Daily from 8 a.m. to dusk
Maps: A trail map is available at www.dcr.virginia.gov/state_parks; maps are available at the entrance gate and at the Environmental Education Center.
Trail contact: Mason Neck State Park, 7301 High Point Rd., Lorton, VA 22079-4010; (703) 339-2385 or (703) 339-2380 (environmental center); www.dcr .virginia.gov/state_parks/mas .shtml

Finding the trailhead: From I-495, take I-95 south toward Richmond. Take exit 166A/Fairfax County Parkway and continue toward Fort Belvoir. Turn right at Telegraph Road, which, after about 1 mile, will turn slightly left and become Old Colchester Road. Turn left at Gunston Road and continue for about 3 miles to High Point Road. Turn right onto High Point Road and drive about 1 mile to the park entrance. Enter the park and follow the road to the environmental center, where the trail begins. GPS: N38 38.664' / W77 11.895'

The Hike

Mason Neck is a peninsula formed by Pohick Bay, Belmont Bay, and the Potomac River, and is home to many types of birds including herons, bald eagles, and swans. It is adjacent to Mason Neck National Wildlife Refuge. The park has a series of trails, all very well marked. Several programs are offered throughout the year, including bald eagle–watching and birding walks, campfire talks, and animal tracking. The Environmental Education Center is surrounded by butterfly gardens, which create a spectacular show in summertime.

The Beach Trail follows the water's edge to a set of stairs leading to a small beach. (Swimming is not allowed.) The Beach Trail joins the interpretive Bayview Trail. This loop goes along the bay, past American holly trees, and then through marshland. Several signs along the way explain the natural history of the area.

The Wilson Spring Trail heads away from the water into the woods and connects to the Dogue Trail, named for the Native Americans who used to live here. It is thought that Captain John Smith explored this area and met with this tribe.

Nearby is Gunston Hall, home of George Mason, which is open to visitors. For more information, visit www.gunstonhall.org.

Miles and Directions

0.0 Park at the Environmental Education Center. There are restrooms here. Start the route by heading around the building and walk to the left along the Beach Trail (green markers).

0.2 From the Beach Trail, join the Bayview Trail (red markers).

0.9 Join the Wilson Spring Trail (yellow markers).

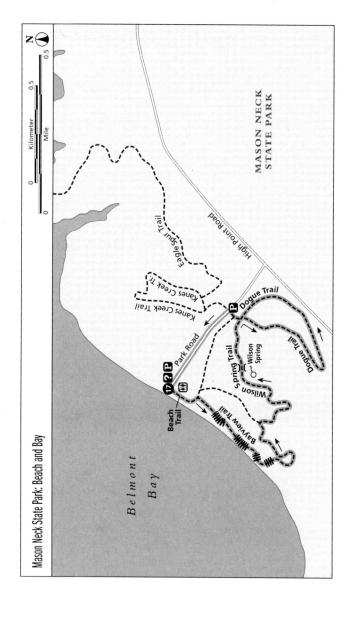

Mason Neck State Park: Beach and Bay

N

Belmont Bay

MASON NECK STATE PARK

Kilometer   0.5
0
Mile   0.5
0

Kanes Creek Trail

Kanes Creek Tr.

Eagle Spur Trail

Park Road

High Point Road

Dogue Trail

P

Wilson Spring Trail

Wilson Spring

Bayview Trail

Beach Trail

P 1/2

1.4 The Wilson Spring Trail ends at a small parking lot. Join the Dogue Trail (orange markers), which loops around and back to the parking lot. Follow the Dogue Trail in a counterclockwise direction.

2.3 From the parking lot at the end of the Dogue Trail, walk out to the park road. Turn left and walk back toward the Environmental Education Center.

2.6 Arrive back at the trailhead and environmental center parking lot.

18 Mason Neck State Park: Kanes Creek

Popular with birders, this hike focuses on the Kanes Creek area, an offshoot of Belmont Bay. Look for bald eagles, herons, and osprey on your hike, especially as you get closer to the water.

Distance: 3.5-mile lollipop
Approximate hiking time: 2.5 hours
Difficulty: Moderate
Trail surface: Natural surface
Best seasons: Year-round
Other trail users: Runners
Canine compatibility: Leashed dogs permitted
Fees and permits: A small fee per car on weekdays; slightly higher per car on weekends
Schedule: Daily from 8 a.m. to dusk

Maps: A trail map is available at www.dcr.virginia.gov/state_parks; maps are available at the entrance gate and at the Environmental Education Center.
Trail contact: Mason Neck State Park, 7301 High Point Rd., Lorton, VA 22079-4010; (703) 339-2385 or (703) 339-2380 (environmental center); www.dcr .virginia.gov/state_parks/mas .shtm

Finding the trailhead: From I-495, take I-95 south toward Richmond. Take exit 166A/Fairfax County Parkway toward Fort Belvoir. Turn right at Telegraph Road, which, after about 1 mile, will turn slightly left and become Old Colchester Road. Turn left at Gunston Road and follow Gunston for about 3 miles to High Point Road. Turn right onto High Point Road and drive about 1 mile to the park entrance gate. After entering the park, follow the road to the first small parking lot on your left at the entrance to the Dogue Trail. GPS: N38 38.452' / W77 11.702'

The Hike

Mason Neck State Park came about when, in 1965, two bald eagle sightings occurred and the Mason Neck Conservation Committee was established. The area had been used for logging during the nineteenth and early twentieth centuries and the removal of hardwoods, along with the use of the pesticide DDT, had driven the bald eagles away. When the two birds were sighted, the committee petitioned the Commonwealth of Virginia to purchase the land and create a park to preserve the area from development. The park is now part of the Virginia state park system and has an active heron rookery. It is also one of the best places in the Washington, D.C. area to see a bald eagle.

This beautiful walk in the woods goes through thick hardwood forest and past a few wildlife protected areas. Keep an eye out for deer and fox on the trail. At the end of the Eagle Spur Trail, there is a bird blind, a small structure built especially to view wildlife without being seen. Be careful if you go into the blind as it is also a popular spot for hornets! The blind overlooks Kane Creek. You might also see kayaks and canoes, as this is a popular water recreation area. Look for great blue heron, Canada geese, and bald eagles.

Miles and Directions

0.0 Cross the road from the parking lot and enter at the trailhead directly across from the lot—this is the end of the Wilson Spring Trail (yellow markers). Follow this to the Kanes Creek Trail (blue markers).

0.1 Bear left and follow the Kanes Creek loop till it joins the Eagle Spur Trail.

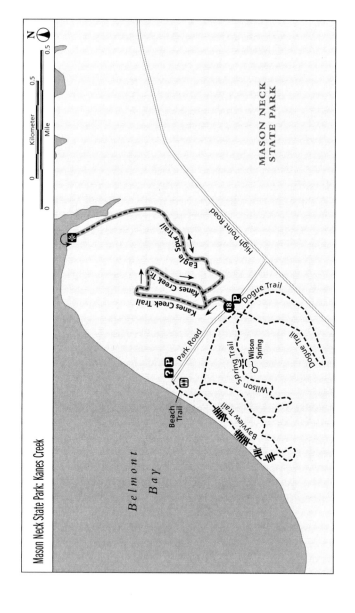

Mason Neck State Park: Kanes Creek

N

Belmont Bay

Beach Trail

Park Road

Kanes Creek Trail

Kanes Creek Trl.

Eagle Spur Trail

High Point Road

Dogue Trail

Wilson Spring Trail

Wilson Spring

Bayview Trail

Dogue Trail

MASON NECK STATE PARK

Kilometer
0   0.5

Mile
0   0.5

1.0 Turn left onto the Eagle Spur Trail (white markers). Follow this till it ends at Kanes Creek. Enjoy the views from the bird blind, then retrace your steps back toward the Kanes Creek Trail.

2.2 Join the Kanes Creek Trail again, turning left.

3.4 Turn left onto the Wilson Spring Trail, heading back to the road and parking lot.

3.5 Arrive back at the trailhead and the parking lot.

19 Belle Haven to Old Town

Follow the marshes along the Potomac River to Old Town Alexandria. Spend some time walking through the streets of this historic city before heading back on the Mount Vernon Trail. The hike can be done in reverse, but parking in Old Town is not as easy. If you start in Old Town, join the trail at Union Street and Jefferson Street, and head south.

Distance: 4.2-mile lollipop (longer if time is spent walking around Old Town)

Approximate hiking time: 3 hours; more if extra time is spent in Old Town

Difficulty: Moderate

Trail surface: Mostly paved; some gravel

Best seasons: Year-round

Other trail users: Cyclists, runners

Canine compatibility: Leashed dogs permitted

Fees and permits: None

Schedule: Trail always open; parking lot closes at dusk

Maps: A map of the Mount Vernon Trail can be found at www .nps.gov/gwmp

Special considerations: Please yield to cyclists and runners if they need to pass. The trail can get very crowded on weekends.

Trail contact: George Washington Memorial Parkway Headquarters, Turkey Run Park, McLean, VA 22101; (703) 289-2500; www.nps.gov/gwmp

Finding the trailhead: On the George Washington Memorial Parkway heading south from Alexandria and the Capital Beltway, turn left into the parking lot for Belle Haven Park and Marina. This hike begins on the Mount Vernon Trail, which runs between the parking lot and the river. GPS: N38 46.730' / W77 03.101'

The Hike

The 17-mile-long Mount Vernon Trail begins at the home of George Washington in Mount Vernon and parallels the Potomac River north to Theodore Roosevelt Island. This portion of the trail starts at the Belle Haven marina, where sailboats, canoes, and kayaks can be rented.

Heading north from Belle Haven, the river will be on your right and the George Washington Memorial Parkway on the left. The trail follows marshland at the edge of the river. Look for ducks and geese, especially in spring and fall. The abundance of honeysuckle vines bloom in late summer and perfume the air.

As you look across the river from Belle Haven, the large complex you see is the National Harbor, a new shopping and dining complex built as part of the revitalization of southwest D.C. You can also see the Woodrow Wilson Bridge.

Before passing under the bridge, turn right at the sign for Jones Point Lighthouse. This doesn't look like most lighthouses, as the beacon light is very short and sits on top of a small white cottage. The light worked from 1856 to 1925, warning sailors of the sandbars along this section of the river. It also marks the southwestern-most corner of the original District of Columbia (land was given back to Virginia in 1847). The park around the lighthouse was a popular place for picnicking, boating, fishing, and, in the winter, ice skating. A renewal project is underway. You can take a short trail down to the river's edge to look for waterfowl, such as ducks, geese, and possibly bald eagles.

From Jones Point, you can rejoin the trail into Old Town without returning all the way to the main trail.

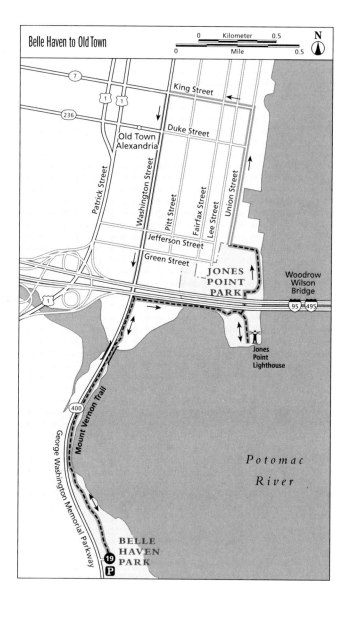

Belle Haven to Old Town

King Street

Duke Street

Old Town Alexandria

Patrick Street

Washington Street

Pitt Street

Fairfax Street

Lee Street

Union Street

Jefferson Street

Green Street

JONES POINT PARK

Woodrow Wilson Bridge

95 495

Jones Point Lighthouse

George Washington Memorial Parkway

Mount Vernon Trail

400

Potomac River

BELLE HAVEN PARK

19 P

0 Kilometer 0.5

0 Mile 0.5

N

Follow the signs for Union Street and head into town. At the corner of Jefferson Street, the path ends and you will be walking on city streets. Follow Union Street to King Street. Spend as much time as you like visiting the shops and restaurants along King Street and through the neighborhood. Historic sites in the area include Christ Church, Gadsby's Tavern, and the Lyceum. For more information, visit www .visitalexandriava.com.

When you're ready to return, walk up to Washington Street and head south on the sidewalk to rejoin the trail where you turned off for Jones Point.

Miles and Directions

0.0 Park at the Belle Haven marina parking lot. Head north on the Mount Vernon Trail, with the river on your right.

0.2 Turn right at the sign to follow the spur path to Jones Point Park.

1.2 Turn right onto a gravel path toward the lighthouse.

1.4 Arrive at the Jones Point Lighthouse. Return to the main paved path and head north, following signs for Union Street.

2.3 Arrive in Old Town Alexandria at the intersection of Union Street and King Street. When you are done exploring Old Town, walk away from the river on King Street to Washington Street and turn left onto the Mount Vernon Trail.

4.2 Arrive back at the trailhead in the Belle Haven parking lot.

20 Belle Haven to Dyke Marsh

Visit one of the area's largest freshwater tidal marshes. Dyke Marsh is home to almost 400 plant species and is popular with birders.

Distance: 3.5 miles total, combining two out-and-back sections
Approximate hiking time: 2 hours
Difficulty: Easy
Trail surface: Boardwalks, paved trail, and natural surfaces
Best seasons: Year-round
Other trail users: Cyclists, runners on the Mount Vernon Trail portion only

Canine compatibility: Dogs not permitted
Fees and permits: None
Schedule: Trail always open; parking lot closes at dusk
Maps: See www.nps.gov/gwmp for a Mount Vernon Trail map.
Trail contact: George Washington Memorial Parkway Headquarters, Turkey Run Park, McLean, VA 22101; (703) 289-2500; www.nps.gov/gwmp

Finding the trailhead: From the George Washington Memorial Parkway heading south out of Alexandria, turn left into the parking lot for Belle Haven Park and Marina. The trailhead is at the parking lot. GPS: N38 46.730' / W77 03.101'

The Hike

Leave the city behind as you enter Dyke Marsh Wildlife Preserve, a large freshwater tidal wetland. The area has open water, marsh, and swamp, and is home to many plants and animals. Follow the "Haul Road" trail into the marsh. The river soon comes into view on your left as you pass by boats anchored around the Belle Haven Marina. As you make your way farther out into the marsh, you can hear the noise

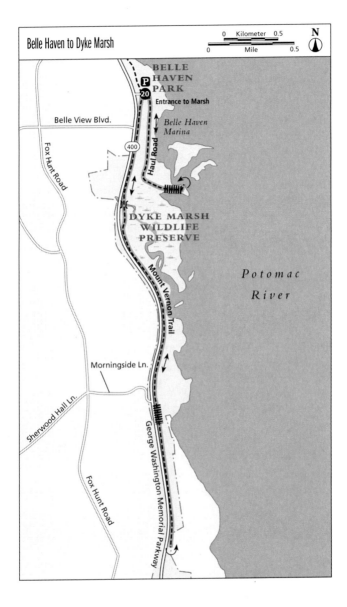

Belle Haven to Dyke Marsh

0 Kilometer 0.5
0 Mile 0.5

N

BELLE
HAVEN
PARK

P
20

Entrance to Marsh

Belle View Blvd.

Belle Haven
Marina

Fox Hunt Road

400

Haul Road

DYKE MARSH
WILDLIFE
PRESERVE

Mount Vernon Trail

Potomac
River

Morningside Ln.

Sherwood Hall Ln.

Fox Hunt Road

George Washington Memorial Parkway

of the city disappear and feel a sense of calm descend. At the very end of the boardwalk is a field of narrow-leafed cattails that bloom in June.

Bird walks are offered by the Friends of Dyke Marsh every Sunday morning at 8 a.m. Commonly seen birds include osprey, egrets, ducks, and flycatchers. Listen too for the mournful cry of the red-winged blackbird. Also living in the area are deer, river otters, rabbits, and beavers.

Return to the beginning of the trail and turn left to follow the Mount Vernon Trail south, traveling through another portion of the marsh. There are cyclists and runners on this busier section, but the trail eventually leads to a section of the marsh. Walk onto the boardwalks; interpretive signs explain what you might see in this area.

Dyke Marsh is administered by the National Park Service and has been officially protected by Congress as a precious ecosystem. The preserve is part of the Virginia Birding and Wildlife Coastal Trail, Mason Neck Loop, developed by the Virginia Department of Game and Inland Fisheries.

Miles and Directions

- **0.0** Start at the Belle Haven Park parking lot. Walk south to the entrance road and turn left and then right into the entrance to the Dyke Marsh Wildlife Preserve.
- **0.1** Follow Haul Road into the preserve.
- **0.8** Reach the overlook at the end of the Haul Road boardwalk. Retrace your steps back to the entrance of the marsh.
- **1.6** Turn left on the marina entrance road, then left onto the Mount Vernon Trail. Head south on the Mount Vernon Trail.
- **2.6** Reach the end of the marsh boardwalk on the Mount Vernon Trail. Turn around and retrace your steps to the parking lot.
- **3.5** Arrive back at the trailhead and parking lot.

About the Author

Louise Baxter is a freelance writer living in the Washington, D.C. area. Her articles have appeared in the *Washington Post, Travel Weekly,* condenast.com, and other publications. She writes about the mid-Atlantic region covering travel-related subjects. She also spent eleven years working in the tour and travel field, planning and operating tours throughout North America.

AMERICAN HIKING SOCIETY

Because you
hike.
We're with you
every step of the way

American Hiking Society gives voice to the more than 75 million Americans who hike and is the only national organization that promotes and protects foot trails, the natural areas that surround them, and the hiking experience. Our work is inspiring and challenging, and is built on three pillars:

Volunteerism and Stewardship
We organize and coordinate nationally recognized programs—including Volunteer Vacations, National Trails Day ®, and the National Trails Fund—that help keep our trails open, safe, and enjoyable.

Policy and Advocacy
We work with Congress and federal agencies to ensure funding for trails, the preservation of natural areas, and the protection of the hiking experience.

Outreach and Education
We expand and support the national constituency of hikers through outreach and education as well as partnerships with other recreation and conservation organizations.

Join us in our efforts. Become an American Hiking Society member today!

American Hiking Society

1422 Fenwick Lane · Silver Spring, MD 20910 · (800) 972-8608
www.AmericanHiking.org · info@AmericanHiking.org